THE NATIONAL SECURITY STRATEGY OF THE UNITED STATES OF AMERICA

THE NATIONAL SECURITY STRATEGY OF THE UNITED STATES OF AMERICA

FRANK COLUMBUS (EDITOR)

Novinka Books
New York

Senior Editors: Susan Boriotti and Donna Dennis
Coordinating Editor: Tatiana Shohov
Office Manager: Annette Hellinger
Graphics: Wanda Serrano
Editorial Production: Maya Columbus, Vladimir Klestov, Matthew Kozlowski,
  Tom Moceri and Anthony T. Sovak
Circulation: Ave Maria Gonzalez, Vera Popovic, Luis Aviles, Raymond Davis,
  Melissa Diaz, Marlene Nunez and Jeannie Pappas
Communications and Acquisitions: Serge P. Shohov
Marketing: Cathy DeGregory

Library of Congress Cataloging-in-Publication Data
Available Upon Request

ISBN: 1-59033-582-1.

Copyright © 2003 by Novinka Books, An Imprint of
  Nova Science Publishers, Inc.
  400 Oser Ave, Suite 1600
  Hauppauge, New York 11788-3619
  Tele. 631-231-7269   Fax 631-231-8175
  e-mail: Novascience@earthlink.net
  Web Site: http://www.novapublishers.com

All rights reserved. No part of this book may be reproduced, stored in a retrieval system or transmitted in any form or by any means: electronic, electrostatic, magnetic, tape, mechanical photocopying, recording or otherwise without permission from the publishers.

The publisher has taken reasonable care in the preparation of this book, but makes no expressed or implied warranty of any kind and assumes no responsibility for any errors or omissions. No liability is assumed for incidental or consequential damages in connection with or arising out of information contained in this book.

This publication is designed to provide accurate and authoritative information with regard to the subject matter covered herein. It is sold with the clear understanding that the publisher is not engaged in rendering legal or any other professional services. If legal or any other expert assistance is required, the services of a competent person should be sought. FROM A DECLARATION OF PARTICIPANTS JOINTLY ADOPTED BY A COMMITTEE OF THE AMERICAN BAR ASSOCIATION AND A COMMITTEE OF PUBLISHERS.

Printed in the United States of America

Contents

Preface		**vii**
PART I. NATIONAL SECURITY STRATEGY OF THE UNITED STATES		**1**
Introduction		**3**
Chapter 1	Overview of America's International Strategy	7
Chapter 2	Champion Aspirations for Human Dignity	9
Chapter 3	Strengthen Alliances to Defeat Global Terrorism and Work to Prevent Attacks against Us and Our Friends	11
Chapter 4	Work with Others to Defuse Regional Conflicts	15
Chapter 5	Prevent Our Enemies from Threatening Us, Our Allies, and Our Friends with Weapons of Mass Destruction	19
Chapter 6	Ignite a New Era of Global Economic Growth through Free Markets and Free Trade	25
Chapter 7	Expand the Circle of Development by Opening Societies and Building the Infrastructure of Democracy	31
Chapter 8	Develop Agendas for Cooperative Action with the Other Main Centers of Global Power	35

Chapter 9	Transform America's National Security Institutions to Meet the Challenges and Opportunities of the Twenty-First Century	**41**
Chapter 10	Strengthening Intelligence to Better Protect America	**47**
PART II. ANALYSES OF PREEMPTIVE FORCE		**53**
Chapter 11	Response to Terrorism: Legal Aspects of the Use of Military Force *David M. Ackerman*	**55**
Chapter 12	U.S. Use of Preemptive Military Force *Richard F. Grimmett*	**59**
Chapter 11	International Law and the Preemptive Use of Force against Iraq *David M. Ackerman*	**65**
Index		**73**

PREFACE

This book presents an astonishing and new national security policy by the White House. For the first time in U.S. history preemptive strikes against real or imagined enemies are broadly justified by the facts of: ever smaller Weapons of Mass Destruction (WMD); widespread hatred of the U.S. (alluded to); apparent willingness of other powers or terrorists to strike first without fear of retaliation (since ghosts are difficult to locate) based on the September 11 attacks. But the preemption option is not limited to terrorists but also to any state which someday may pose a real or perceived threat to U.S. hegemony. Even if one were to accept, and many would not, the proposition that the current U.S. security officials are reasonable and moral individuals, the new strategy could trigger war anytime against any county after a little media warmup. The book is augmented by three analyses relevant to the use of preemptive military force.

Part I.
National Security
Strategy of the United States

INTRODUCTION

The great struggles of the twentieth century between liberty and totalitarianism ended with a decisive victory for the forces of freedom—and a single sustainable model for national success: freedom, democracy, and free enterprise. In the twenty-first century, only nations that share a commitment to protecting basic human rights and guaranteeing political and economic freedom will be able to unleash the potential of their people and assure their future prosperity. People everywhere want to be able to speak freely; choose who will govern them; worship as they please; educate their children—male and female; own property; and enjoy the benefits of their labor. These values of freedom are right and true for every person, in every society—and the duty of protecting these values against their enemies is the common calling of freedom-loving people across the globe and across the ages.

Today, the United States enjoys a position of unparalleled military strength and great economic and political influence. In keeping with our heritage and principles, we do not use our strength to press for unilateral advantage. We seek instead to create a balance of power that favors human freedom: conditions in which all nations and all societies can choose for themselves the rewards and challenges of political and economic liberty. In a world that is safe, people will be able to make their own lives better. We will defend the peace by fighting terrorists and tyrants. We will preserve the peace by building good relations among the great powers. We will extend the peace by encouraging free and open societies on every continent.

Defending our Nation against its enemies is the first and fundamental commitment of the Federal Government. Today, that task has changed dramatically. Enemies in the past needed great armies and great industrial capabilities to endanger America. Now, shadowy networks of individuals can bring great chaos and suffering to our shores for less than it costs to purchase a single tank. Terrorists are organized to penetrate open societies and to turn the power of modern technologies against us.

To defeat this threat we must make use of every tool in our arsenal— military power, better homeland defenses, law enforcement, intelligence, and vigorous efforts to cut off terrorist financing. The war against terrorists of global reach is a global enterprise of uncertain duration. America will help nations that need our assistance in combating terror. And America will hold to account nations that are compromised by terror, including those who harbor terrorists— because the allies of terror are the enemies of civilization. The United States and countries cooperating with us must not allow the terrorists to develop new home bases. Together, we will seek to deny them sanctuary at every turn.

The gravest danger our Nation faces lies at the crossroads of radicalism and technology. Our enemies have openly declared that they are seeking weapons of mass destruction, and evidence indicates that they are doing so with determination. The United States will not allow these efforts to succeed. We will build defenses against ballistic missiles and other means of delivery. We will cooperate with other nations to deny, contain, and curtail our enemies' efforts to acquire dangerous technologies. And, as a matter of common sense and self-defense, America will act against such emerging threats before they are fully formed. We cannot defend America and our friends by hoping for the best. So we must be prepared to defeat our enemies' plans, using the best intelligence and proceeding with deliberation. History will judge harshly those who saw this coming danger but failed to act. In the new world we have entered, the only path to peace and security is the path of action.

As we defend the peace, we will also take advantage of an historic opportunity to preserve the peace. Today, the international community has the best chance since the rise of the nation-state in the seventeenth century to build a world where great powers compete in peace instead of continually prepare for war. Today, the world's great powers find ourselves on the same side— united by common dangers of terrorist violence and chaos. The United States will build on these common interests to promote global security. We are also increasingly united by common values. Russia is in the midst of a hopeful transition, reaching for its democratic future and a partner in the war on terror. Chinese leaders are discovering that economic freedom is the only source of national wealth. In time, they will find that social and political freedom is the only source of national greatness. America will encourage the advancement of democracy and economic openness in both nations, because these are the best foundations for domestic stability and international order. We will strongly resist aggression from other great powers—even as we welcome their peaceful pursuit of prosperity, trade, and cultural advancement.

Finally, the United States will use this moment of opportunity to extend the benefits of freedom across the globe. We will actively work to bring the hope of democracy, development, free markets, and free trade to every corner of the world. The events of September 11, 2001, taught us that weak states, like Afghanistan, can pose as great a danger to our national interests as strong states. Poverty does not make poor people into terrorists and murderers. Yet poverty, weak institutions, and corruption can make weak states vulnerable to terrorist networks and drug cartels within their borders.

The United States will stand beside any nation determined to build a better future by seeking the rewards of liberty for its people. Free trade and free markets have proven their ability to lift whole societies out of poverty—so the United States will work with individual nations, entire regions, and the entire global trading community to build a world that trades in freedom and therefore grows in prosperity. The United States will deliver greater development assistance through the New Millennium Challenge Account to nations that govern justly, invest in their people, and encourage economic freedom. We will also continue to lead the world in efforts to reduce the terrible toll of HIV/AIDS and other infectious diseases.

In building a balance of power that favors freedom, the United States is guided by the conviction that all nations have important responsibilities. Nations that enjoy freedom must actively fight terror. Nations that depend on international stability must help prevent the spread of weapons of mass destruction. Nations that seek international aid must govern themselves wisely, so that aid is well spent. For freedom to thrive, accountability must be expected and required.

We are also guided by the conviction that no nation can build a safer, better world alone. Alliances and multilateral institutions can multiply the strength of freedom-loving nations. The United States is committed to lasting institutions like the United Nations, the World Trade Organization, the Organization of American States, and NATO as well as other long-standing alliances. Coalitions of the willing can augment these permanent institutions. In all cases, international obligations are to be taken seriously. They are not to be undertaken symbolically to rally support for an ideal without furthering its attainment.

Freedom is the non-negotiable demand of human dignity; the birthright of every person—in every civilization. Throughout history, freedom has been threatened by war and terror; it has been challenged by the clashing wills of powerful states and the evil designs of tyrants; and it has been tested by widespread poverty and disease. Today, humanity holds in its hands the opportunity to further freedom's triumph over all these foes. The United States welcomes our responsibility to lead in this great mission.

George W. Bush
THE WHITE HOUSE,
September 17, 2002

Chapter 1

OVERVIEW OF AMERICA'S INTERNATIONAL STRATEGY

> *"Our Nation's cause has always been larger than our Nation's defense. We fight, as we always fight, for a just peace—a peace that favors liberty. We will defend the peace against the threats from terrorists and tyrants. We will preserve the peace by building good relations among the great powers. And we will extend the peace by encouraging free and open societies on every continent."*
>
> President Bush
> West Point, New York
> June 1, 2002

The United States possesses unprecedented— and unequaled—strength and influence in the world. Sustained by faith in the principles of liberty, and the value of a free society, this position comes with unparalleled responsibilities, obligations, and opportunity. The great strength of this nation must be used to promote a balance of power that favors freedom.

For most of the twentieth century, the world was divided by a great struggle over ideas: destructive totalitarian visions versus freedom and equality.

That great struggle is over. The militant visions of class, nation, and race which promised utopia and delivered misery have been defeated and discredited. America is now threatened less by conquering states than we are by failing ones. We are menaced less by fleets and armies than by catastrophic technologies in the hands of the embittered few. We must defeat these threats to our Nation, allies, and friends.

This is also a time of opportunity for America. We will work to translate this moment of influence into decades of peace, prosperity, and liberty. The U.S. national security strategy will be based on a distinctly American internationalism that reflects the union of our values and our national interests. The aim of this strategy is to help make the world not just safer but better. Our goals on the path to progress are clear: political and economic freedom, peaceful relations with other states, and respect for human dignity.

And this path is not America's alone. It is open to all. To achieve these goals, the United States will:

- champion aspirations for human dignity;

- strengthen alliances to defeat global terrorism and work to prevent attacks against us and our friends;

- work with others to defuse regional conflicts;

- prevent our enemies from threatening us, our allies, and our friends, with weapons of mass destruction;

- ignite a new era of global economic growth through free markets and free trade;

- expand the circle of development by opening societies and building the infrastructure of democracy;

- develop agendas for cooperative action with other main centers of global power; and

- transform America's national security institutions to meet the challenges and opportunities of the twenty-first century.

Chapter 2

CHAMPION ASPIRATIONS FOR HUMAN DIGNITY

> *"Some worry that it is somehow undiplomatic or impolite to speak the language of right and wrong. I disagree. Different circumstances require different methods, but not different moralities."*
>
> President Bush
> West Point, New York
> June 1, 2002

In pursuit of our goals, our first imperative is to clarify what we stand for: the United States must defend liberty and justice because these principles are right and true for all people everywhere. No nation owns these aspirations, and no nation is exempt from them. Fathers and mothers in all societies want their children to be educated and to live free from poverty and violence. No people on earth yearn to be oppressed, aspire to servitude, or eagerly await the midnight knock of the secret police.

America must stand firmly for the nonnegotiable demands of human dignity: the rule of law; limits on the absolute power of the state; free speech; freedom of worship; equal justice; respect for women; religious and ethnic tolerance; and respect for private property.

These demands can be met in many ways. America's constitution has served us well. Many other nations, with different histories and cultures, facing different circumstances, have successfully incorporated these core principles into their own systems of governance. History has not been kind to those nations which ignored or flouted the rights and aspirations of their people.

America's experience as a great multi-ethnic democracy affirms our conviction that people of many heritages and faiths can live and prosper in peace. Our own history is a long struggle to live up to our ideals. But even in our worst moments, the principles enshrined in the Declaration of Independence were there to guide us. As a result, America is not just a stronger, but is a freer and more just society.

Today, these ideals are a lifeline to lonely defenders of liberty. And when openings arrive, we can encourage change—as we did in central and eastern Europe between 1989 and 1991, or in Belgrade in 2000. When we see democratic processes take hold among our friends in Taiwan or in the Republic of Korea, and see elected leaders replace generals in Latin America and Africa, we see examples of how authoritarian systems can evolve, marrying local history and traditions with the principles we all cherish.

Embodying lessons from our past and using the opportunity we have today, the national security strategy of the United States must start from these core beliefs and look outward for possibilities to expand liberty.

Our principles will guide our government's decisions about international cooperation, the character of our foreign assistance, and the allocation of resources. They will guide our actions and our words in international bodies. We will:

- speak out honestly about violations of the nonnegotiable demands of human dignity using our voice and vote in international institutions to advance freedom;

- use our foreign aid to promote freedom and support those who struggle non-violently for it, ensuring that nations moving toward democracy are rewarded for the steps they take;

- make freedom and the development of democratic institutions key themes in our bilateral relations, seeking solidarity and cooperation from other democracies while we press governments that deny human rights to move toward a better future; and

- take special efforts to promote freedom of religion and conscience and defend it from encroachment by repressive governments.

We will champion the cause of human dignity and oppose those who resist it.

Chapter 3

STRENGTHEN ALLIANCES TO DEFEAT GLOBAL TERRORISM AND WORK TO PREVENT ATTACKS AGAINST US AND OUR FRIENDS

> *"Just three days removed from these events, Americans do not yet have the distance of history. But our responsibility to history is already clear: to answer these attacks and rid the world of evil. War has been waged against us by stealth and deceit and murder. This nation is peaceful, but fierce when stirred to anger. The conflict was begun on the timing and terms of others. It will end in a way, and at an hour, of our choosing."*
>
> President Bush
> Washington, D.C. (The National Cathedral)
> September 14, 2001

The United States of America is fighting a war against terrorists of global reach. The enemy is not a single political regime or person or religion or ideology. The enemy is terrorism— premeditated, politically motivated violence perpetrated against innocents.

In many regions, legitimate grievances prevent the emergence of a lasting peace. Such grievances deserve to be, and must be, addressed within a political process. But no cause justifies terror. The United States will make no concessions to terrorist demands and strike no deals with them. We make no distinction between terrorists and those who knowingly harbor or provide aid to them.

The struggle against global terrorism is different from any other war in our history. It will be fought on many fronts against a particularly elusive enemy over an extended period of time. Progress will come through the persistent accumulation of successes—some seen, some unseen.

Today our enemies have seen the results of what civilized nations can, and will, do against regimes that harbor, support, and use terrorism to achieve their political goals. Afghanistan has been liberated; coalition forces continue to hunt down the Taliban and al-Qaida. But it is not only this battlefield on which we will engage terrorists. Thousands of trained terrorists remain at large with cells in North America, South America, Europe, Africa, the Middle East, and across Asia.

Our priority will be first to disrupt and destroy terrorist organizations of global reach and attack their leadership; command, control, and communications; material support; and finances. This will have a disabling effect upon the terrorists' ability to plan and operate.

We will continue to encourage our regional partners to take up a coordinated effort that isolates the terrorists. Once the regional campaign localizes the threat to a particular state, we will help ensure the state has the military, law enforcement, political, and financial tools necessary to finish the task.

The United States will continue to work with our allies to disrupt the financing of terrorism. We will identify and block the sources of funding for terrorism, freeze the assets of terrorists and those who support them, deny terrorists access to the international financial system, protect legitimate charities from being abused by terrorists, and prevent the movement of terrorists' assets through alternative financial networks.

However, this campaign need not be sequential to be effective, the cumulative effect across all regions will help achieve the results we seek. We will disrupt and destroy terrorist organizations by:

- direct and continuous action using all the elements of national and international power. Our immediate focus will be those terrorist organizations of global reach and any terrorist or state sponsor of terrorism which attempts to gain or use weapons of mass destruction or their precursors;

- defending the United States, the American people, and our interests at home and abroad by identifying and destroying the threat before it reaches our borders. While the United States will constantly strive to enlist the support of the international community, we will not hesitate to act alone, if necessary, to exercise our right of selfdefense by acting preemptively against such terrorists, to prevent them from doing harm against our people and our country; and

- denying further sponsorship, support, and sanctuary to terrorists by convincing or compelling states to accept their sovereign responsibilities. We will also wage a war of ideas to win the battle against international terrorism. This includes:

- using the full influence of the United States, and working closely with allies and friends, to make clear that all acts of terrorism are illegitimate so that terrorism will be viewed in the same light as slavery, piracy, or genocide: behavior that no respectable government can condone or support and all must oppose;

- supporting moderate and modern government, especially in the Muslim world, to ensure that the conditions and ideologies that promote terrorism do not find fertile ground in any nation;

- diminishing the underlying conditions that spawn terrorism by enlisting the international community to focus its efforts and resources on areas most at risk; and

- using effective public diplomacy to promote the free flow of information and ideas to kindle the hopes and aspirations of freedom of those in societies ruled by the sponsors of global terrorism.

While we recognize that our best defense is a good offense, we are also strengthening America's homeland security to protect against and deter attack. This Administration has proposed the largest government reorganization since the Truman Administration created the National Security Council and the Department of Defense. Centered on a new Department of Homeland Security and including a new unified military command and a fundamental reordering of the FBI, our comprehensive plan to secure the homeland encompasses every level of government and the cooperation of the public and the private sector.

This strategy will turn adversity into opportunity. For example, emergency management systems will be better able to cope not just with terrorism but with all hazards. Our medical system will be strengthened to manage not just bioterror, but all infectious diseases and mass-casualty dangers. Our border controls will not just stop terrorists, but improve the efficient movement of legitimate traffic.

While our focus is protecting America, we know that to defeat terrorism in today's globalized world we need support from our allies and friends. Wherever possible, the United States will rely on regional organizations and state powers to meet their obligations to fight terrorism. Where governments find the fight against terrorism beyond their capacities, we will match their willpower and their resources with whatever help we and our allies can provide.

As we pursue the terrorists in Afghanistan, we will continue to work with international organizations such as the United Nations, as well as non-governmental organizations, and other countries to provide the humanitarian, political, economic, and security assistance necessary to rebuild Afghanistan so that it will never again abuse its people, threaten its neighbors, and provide a haven for terrorists.

In the war against global terrorism, we will never forget that we are ultimately fighting for our democratic values and way of life. Freedom and fear are at war, and there will be no quick or easy end to this conflict. In leading the campaign against terrorism, we are forging new, productive international relationships and redefining existing ones in ways that meet the challenges of the twenty-first century.

Chapter 4

WORK WITH OTHERS TO DEFUSE REGIONAL CONFLICTS

"We build a world of justice, or we will live in a world of coercion. The magnitude of our shared responsibilities makes our disagreements look so small."

President Bush
Berlin, Germany
May 23, 2002

Concerned nations must remain actively engaged in critical regional disputes to avoid explosive escalation and minimize human suffering. In an increasingly interconnected world, regional crisis can strain our alliances, rekindle rivalries among the major powers, and create horrifying affronts to human dignity. When violence erupts and states falter, the United States will work with friends and partners to alleviate suffering and restore stability.

No doctrine can anticipate every circumstance in which U.S. action—direct or indirect—is warranted. We have finite political, economic, and military resources to meet our global priorities. The United States will approach each case with these strategic principles in mind:

- The United States should invest time and resources into building international relationships and institutions that can help manage local crises when they emerge.

- The United States should be realistic about its ability to help those who are unwilling or unready to help themselves. Where and when people are ready to do their part, we will be willing to move decisively.

The Israeli-Palestinian conflict is critical because of the toll of human suffering, because of America's close relationship with the state of Israel and key Arab states, and because of that region's importance to other global priorities of the United States. There can be no peace for either side without freedom for both sides. America stands committed to an independent and democratic Palestine, living beside Israel in peace and security. Like all other people, Palestinians deserve a government that serves their interests and listens to their voices. The United States will continue to encourage all parties to step up to their responsibilities as we seek a just and comprehensive settlement to the conflict.

The United States, the international donor community, and the World Bank stand ready to work with a reformed Palestinian government on economic development, increased humanitarian assistance, and a program to establish, finance, and monitor a truly independent judiciary. If Palestinians embrace democracy, and the rule of law, confront corruption, and firmly reject terror, they can count on American support for the creation of a Palestinian state.

Israel also has a large stake in the success of a democratic Palestine. Permanent occupation threatens Israel's identity and democracy. So the United States continues to challenge Israeli leaders to take concrete steps to support the emergence of a viable, credible Palestinian state. As there is progress towards security, Israel forces need to withdraw fully to positions they held prior to September 28, 2000. And consistent with the recommendations of the Mitchell Committee, Israeli settlement activity in the occupied territories must stop. As violence subsides, freedom of movement should be restored, permitting innocent Palestinians to resume work and normal life. The United States can play a crucial role but, ultimately, lasting peace can only come when Israelis and Palestinians resolve the issues and end the conflict between them.

In South Asia, the United States has also emphasized the need for India and Pakistan to resolve their disputes. This Administration invested time and resources building strong bilateral relations with India and Pakistan. These strong relations then gave us leverage to play a constructive role when tensions in the region became acute. With Pakistan, our bilateral relations have been bolstered by Pakistan's choice to join the war against terror and move toward building a more open and tolerant society. The Administration sees India's potential to become one of the great democratic powers of the twenty-first century and has worked hard to transform our relationship accordingly. Our involvement in this regional dispute, building on earlier investments in bilateral relations, looks first to concrete steps by India and Pakistan that can help defuse military confrontation.

Indonesia took courageous steps to create a working democracy and respect for the rule of law. By tolerating ethnic minorities, respecting the rule of law, and accepting open markets, Indonesia may be able to employ the engine of opportunity that has helped lift some of its neighbors out of poverty and desperation. It is the initiative by Indonesia that allows U.S. assistance to make a difference.

In the Western Hemisphere we have formed flexible coalitions with countries that share our priorities, particularly Mexico, Brazil, Canada, Chile, and Colombia. Together we will promote a truly democratic hemisphere where our integration advances security, prosperity, opportunity, and hope. We will work with regional institutions, such as the Summit of the Americas process, the Organization of American States (OAS), and the Defense Ministerial of the Americas for the benefit of the entire hemisphere.

Parts of Latin America confront regional conflict, especially arising from the violence of drug cartels and their accomplices. This conflict and unrestrained narcotics trafficking could imperil the health and security of the United States. Therefore we have developed an active strategy to help the Andean nations adjust their economies, enforce their laws, defeat terrorist organizations, and cut off the supply of drugs, while—as important—we work to reduce the demand for drugs in our own country.

In Colombia, we recognize the link between terrorist and extremist groups that challenge the security of the state and drug trafficking activities that help finance the operations of such groups. We are working to help Colombia defend its democratic institutions and defeat illegal armed groups of both the left and right by extending effective sovereignty over the entire national territory and provide basic security to the Colombian people.

In Africa, promise and opportunity sit side by side with disease, war, and desperate poverty. This threatens both a core value of the United States— preserving human dignity—and our strategic priority—combating global terror. American interests and American principles, therefore, lead in the same direction: we will work with others for an African continent that lives in liberty, peace, and growing prosperity. Together with our European allies, we must help strengthen Africa's fragile states, help build indigenous capability to secure porous borders, and help build up the law enforcement and intelligence infrastructure to deny havens for terrorists.

An ever more lethal environment exists in Africa as local civil wars spread beyond borders to create regional war zones. Forming coalitions of the willing and cooperative security arrangements are key to confronting these emerging transnational threats.

Africa's great size and diversity requires a security strategy that focuses on bilateral engagement and builds coalitions of the willing. This Administration will focus on three interlocking strategies for the region:

- countries with major impact on their neighborhood such as South Africa, Nigeria, Kenya, and Ethiopia are anchors for regional engagement and require focused attention;

- coordination with European allies and international institutions is essential for constructive conflict mediation and successful peace operations; and

- Africa's capable reforming states and sub-regional organizations must be strengthened as the primary means to address transnational threats on a sustained basis.

Ultimately the path of political and economic freedom presents the surest route to progress in sub-Saharan Africa, where most wars are conflicts over material resources and political access often tragically waged on the basis of ethnic and religious difference. The transition to the African Union with its stated commitment to good governance and a common responsibility for democratic political systems offers opportunities to strengthen democracy on the continent.

Chapter 5

PREVENT OUR ENEMIES FROM THREATENING US, OUR ALLIES, AND OUR FRIENDS WITH WEAPONS OF MASS DESTRUCTION

> *"The gravest danger to freedom lies at the crossroads of radicalism and technology. When the spread of chemical and biological and nuclear weapons, along with ballistic missile technology—when that occurs, even weak states and small groups could attain a catastrophic power to strike great nations. Our enemies have declared this very intention, and have been caught seeking these terrible weapons. They want the capability to blackmail us, or to harm us, or to harm our friends—and we will oppose them with all our power."*
>
> President Bush
> West Point, New York
> June 1, 2002

The nature of the Cold War threat required the United States—with our allies and friends—to emphasize deterrence of the enemy's use of force, producing a grim strategy of mutual assured destruction. With the collapse of the Soviet Union and the end of the Cold War, our security environment has undergone profound transformation.

Having moved from confrontation to cooperation as the hallmark of our relationship with Russia, the dividends are evident: an end to the balance of terror that divided us; an historic reduction in the nuclear arsenals on both sides; and cooperation in areas such as counterterrorism and missile defense that until recently were inconceivable.

But new deadly challenges have emerged from rogue states and terrorists. None of these contemporary threats rival the sheer destructive power that was arrayed against us by the Soviet Union. However, the nature and motivations of these new adversaries, their determination to obtain destructive powers hitherto available only to the world's strongest states, and the greater likelihood that they will use weapons of mass destruction against us, make today's security environment more complex and dangerous.

In the 1990s we witnessed the emergence of a small number of rogue states that, while different in important ways, share a number of attributes. These states:

- brutalize their own people and squander their national resources for the personal gain of the rulers;

- display no regard for international law, threaten their neighbors, and callously violate international treaties to which they are party;

- are determined to acquire weapons of mass destruction, along with other advanced military technology, to be used as threats or offensively to achieve the aggressive designs of these regimes;

- sponsor terrorism around the globe; and

- reject basic human values and hate the United States and everything for which it stands.

At the time of the Gulf War, we acquired irrefutable proof that Iraq's designs were not limited to the chemical weapons it had used against Iran and its own people, but also extended to the acquisition of nuclear weapons and biological agents. In the past decade North Korea has become the world's principal purveyor of ballistic missiles, and has tested increasingly capable missiles while developing its own WMD arsenal. Other rogue regimes seek nuclear, biological, and chemical weapons as well. These states' pursuit of, and global trade in, such weapons has become a looming threat to all nations.

We must be prepared to stop rogue states and their terrorist clients before they are able to threaten or use weapons of mass destruction against the United States and our allies and friends. Our response must take full advantage of strengthened alliances, the establishment of new partnerships with former adversaries, innovation in the use of military forces, modern technologies, including the development of an effective missile defense system, and increased emphasis on intelligence collection and analysis.

Our comprehensive strategy to combat WMD includes:

- *Proactive counterproliferation efforts.* We must deter and defend against the threat before it is unleashed. We must ensure that key capabilities—detection, active and passive defenses, and counterforce capabilities—are integrated into our defense transformation and our homeland security systems. Counterproliferation must also be integrated into the doctrine, training, and equipping of our forces and those of our allies to ensure that we can prevail in any conflict with WMD-armed adversaries.

- *Strengthened nonproliferation efforts to prevent rogue states and terrorists from acquiring the materials, technologies, and expertise necessary for weapons of mass destruction.* We will enhance diplomacy, arms control, multilateral export controls, and threat reduction assistance that impede states and terrorists seeking WMD, and when necessary, interdict enabling technologies and materials. We will continue to build coalitions to support these efforts, encouraging their increased political and financial support for nonproliferation and threat reduction programs. The recent G-8 agreement to commit up to $20 billion to a global partnership against proliferation marks a major step forward.

- *Effective consequence management to respond to the effects of WMD use, whether by terrorists or hostile states.* Minimizing the effects of WMD use against our people will help deter those who possess such weapons and dissuade those who seek to acquire them by persuading enemies that they cannot attain their desired ends. The United States must also be prepared to respond to the effects of WMD use against our forces abroad, and to help friends and allies if they are attacked.

It has taken almost a decade for us to comprehend the true nature of this new threat. Given the goals of rogue states and terrorists, the United States can no longer solely rely on a reactive posture as we have in the past. The inability to deter a potential attacker, the immediacy of today's threats, and the magnitude of potential harm that could be caused by our adversaries' choice of weapons, do not permit that option. We cannot let our enemies strike first.

In the Cold War, especially following the Cuban missile crisis, we faced a generally status quo, risk-averse adversary. Deterrence was an effective defense. But deterrence based only upon the threat of retaliation is less likely to work against leaders of rogue states more willing to take risks, gambling with the lives of their people, and the wealth of their nations.

- In the Cold War, weapons of mass destruction were considered weapons of last resort whose use risked the destruction of those who used them. Today, our enemies see weapons of mass destruction as weapons of choice. For rogue states these weapons are tools of intimidation and military aggression against their neighbors. These weapons may also allow these states to attempt to blackmail the United States and our allies to prevent us from deterring or repelling the aggressive behavior of rogue states. Such states also see these weapons as their best means of overcoming the conventional superiority of the United States.

- Traditional concepts of deterrence will not work against a terrorist enemy whose avowed tactics are wanton destruction and the targeting of innocents; whose so-called soldiers seek martyrdom in death and whose most potent protection is statelessness. The overlap between states that sponsor terror and those that pursue WMD compels us to action.

For centuries, international law recognized that nations need not suffer an attack before they can lawfully take action to defend themselves against forces that present an imminent danger of attack. Legal scholars and international jurists often conditioned the legitimacy of preemption on the existence of an imminent threat—most often a visible mobilization of armies, navies, and air forces preparing to attack.

We must adapt the concept of imminent threat to the capabilities and objectives of today's adversaries. Rogue states and terrorists do not seek to attack us using conventional means. They know such attacks would fail. Instead, they rely on acts of terror and, potentially, the use of weapons of mass destruction—weapons that can be easily concealed, delivered covertly, and used without warning.

The targets of these attacks are our military forces and our civilian population, in direct violation of one of the principal norms of the law of warfare. As was demonstrated by the losses on September 11, 2001, mass civilian casualties is the specific objective of terrorists and these losses would be exponentially more severe if terrorists acquired and used weapons of mass destruction.

The United States has long maintained the option of preemptive actions to counter a sufficient threat to our national security. The greater the threat, the greater is the risk of inaction— and the more compelling the case for taking anticipatory action to defend ourselves, even if uncertainty remains as to the time and place of the enemy's attack. To forestall or prevent such hostile acts by our adversaries, the United States will, if necessary, act preemptively.

The United States will not use force in all cases to preempt emerging threats, nor should nations use preemption as a pretext for aggression. Yet in an age where the enemies of civilization openly and actively seek the world's most destructive technologies, the United States cannot remain idle while dangers gather. We will always proceed deliberately, weighing the consequences of our actions. To support preemptive options, we will:

- build better, more integrated intelligence capabilities to provide timely, accurate information on threats, wherever they may emerge;

- coordinate closely with allies to form a common assessment of the most dangerous threats; and

- continue to transform our military forces to ensure our ability to conduct rapid and precise operations to achieve decisive results.

The purpose of our actions will always be to eliminate a specific threat to the United States or our allies and friends. The reasons for our actions will be clear, the force measured, and the cause just.

Chapter 6

IGNITE A NEW ERA OF GLOBAL ECONOMIC GROWTH THROUGH FREE MARKETS AND FREE TRADE

> *"When nations close their markets and opportunity is hoarded by a privileged few, no amount-no amount-of development aid is ever enough. When nations respect their people, open markets, invest in better health and education, every dollar of aid, every dollar of trade revenue and domestic capital is used more effectively."*
>
> President Bush
Monterrey, Mexico
March 22, 2002

A strong world economy enhances our national security by advancing prosperity and freedom in the rest of the world. Economic growth supported by free trade and free markets creates new jobs and higher incomes. It allows people to lift their lives out of poverty, spurs economic and legal reform, and the fight against corruption, and it reinforces the habits of liberty.

We will promote economic growth and economic freedom beyond America's shores. All governments are responsible for creating their own economic policies and responding to their own economic challenges. We will use our economic engagement with other countries to underscore the benefits of policies that generate higher productivity and sustained economic growth, including:

- pro-growth legal and regulatory policies to encourage business investment, innovation, and entrepreneurial activity;

- tax policies—particularly lower marginal tax rates—that improve incentives for work and investment;

- rule of law and intolerance of corruption so that people are confident that they will be able to enjoy the fruits of their economic endeavors;

- strong financial systems that allow capital to be put to its most efficient use;

- sound fiscal policies to support business activity;

- investments in health and education that improve the well-being and skills of the labor force and population as a whole; and

- free trade that provides new avenues for growth and fosters the diffusion of technologies and ideas that increase productivity and opportunity.

The lessons of history are clear: market economies, not command-and-control economies with the heavy hand of government, are the best way to promote prosperity and reduce poverty. Policies that further strengthen market incentives and market institutions are relevant for all economies—industrialized countries, emerging markets, and the developing world.

A return to strong economic growth in Europe and Japan is vital to U.S. national security interests. We want our allies to have strong economies for their own sake, for the sake of the global economy, and for the sake of global security. European efforts to remove structural barriers in their economies are particularly important in this regard, as are Japan's efforts to end deflation and address the problems of non-performing loans in the Japanese banking system. We will continue to use our regular consultations with Japan and our European partners—including through the Group of Seven (G-7)—to discuss policies they are adopting to promote growth in their economies and support higher global economic growth.

Improving stability in emerging markets is also key to global economic growth. International flows of investment capital are needed to expand the productive potential of these economies. These flows allow emerging markets and developing countries to make the investments that raise living standards and reduce poverty. Our long-term objective should be a world in which all countries have investment-grade credit ratings that allow them access to international capital markets and to invest in their future.

We are committed to policies that will help emerging markets achieve access to larger capital flows at lower cost. To this end, we will continue to pursue reforms aimed at reducing uncertainty in financial markets. We will work actively with other countries, the International Monetary Fund (IMF), and the private sector to implement the G-7 Action Plan negotiated earlier this year for preventing financial crises and more effectively resolving them when they occur.

The best way to deal with financial crises is to prevent them from occurring, and we have encouraged the IMF to improve its efforts doing so. We will continue to work with the IMF to streamline the policy conditions for its lending and to focus its lending strategy on achieving economic growth through sound fiscal and monetary policy, exchange rate policy, and financial sector policy.

The concept of "free trade" arose as a moral principle even before it became a pillar of economics. If you can make something that others value, you should be able to sell it to them. If others make something that you value, you should be able to buy it. This is real freedom, the freedom for a person—or a nation—to make a living. To promote free trade, the Unites States has developed a comprehensive strategy:

- *Seize the global initiative.* The new global trade negotiations we helped launch at Doha in November 2001 will have an ambitious agenda, especially in agriculture, manufacturing, and services, targeted for completion in 2005. The United States has led the way in completing the accession of China and a democratic Taiwan to the World Trade Organization. We will assist Russia's preparations to join the WTO.

- *Press regional initiatives.* The United States and other democracies in the Western Hemisphere have agreed to create the Free Trade Area of the Americas, targeted for completion in 2005. This year the United States will advocate market-access negotiations with its partners, targeted on agriculture, industrial goods, services, investment, and government procurement. We will also offer more opportunity to the poorest continent, Africa, starting with full use of the preferences allowed in the African Growth and Opportunity Act, and leading to free trade.

- *Move ahead with bilateral free trade agreements.* Building on the free trade agreement with Jordan enacted in 2001, the Administration will work this year to complete free trade agreements with Chile and Singapore. Our aim is to achieve free trade agreements with a mix of developed and developing countries in all regions of the world. Initially, Central America, Southern Africa, Morocco, and Australia will be our principal focal points.

- *Renew the executive-congressional partnership.* Every administration's trade strategy depends on a productive partnership with Congress. After a gap of 8 years, the Administration reestablished majority support in the Congress for trade liberalization by passing Trade Promotion Authority and the other market opening measures for developing countries in the Trade Act of 2002. This Administration will work with Congress to enact new bilateral, regional, and global trade agreements that will be concluded under the recently passed Trade Promotion Authority.

- *Promote the connection between trade and development.* Trade policies can help developing countries strengthen property rights, competition, the rule of law, investment, the spread of knowledge, open societies, the efficient allocation of resources, and regional integration—all leading to growth, opportunity, and confidence in developing countries. The United States is implementing The Africa Growth and Opportunity Act to provide market-access for nearly all goods produced in the 35 countries of sub- Saharan Africa. We will make more use of this act and its equivalent for the Caribbean Basin and continue to work with multilateral and regional institutions to help poorer countries take advantage of these opportunities. Beyond market access, the most important area where trade intersects with poverty is in public health. We will ensure that the WTO intellectual property rules are flexible enough to allow developing nations to gain access to critical medicines for extraordinary dangers like HIV/AIDS, tuberculosis, and malaria.

- *Enforce trade agreements and laws against unfair practices.* Commerce depends on the rule of law; international trade depends on enforceable agreements. Our top priorities are to resolve ongoing disputes with the European Union, Canada, and Mexico and to make a global effort to address new technology, science, and health regulations that needlessly impede farm exports and improved agriculture. Laws against unfair trade practices are often abused, but the international community must be able to address genuine concerns about government subsidies and dumping. International industrial espionage which undermines fair competition must be detected and deterred.

- *Help domestic industries and workers adjust.* There is a sound statutory framework for these transitional safeguards which we have used in the agricultural sector and which we are using this year to help the American steel industry. The benefits of free trade depend upon the enforcement of fair trading practices. These safeguards help ensure that the benefits of free trade do not come at the expense of American workers. Trade adjustment assistance will help workers adapt to the change and dynamism of open markets.

- *Protect the environment and workers.* The United States must foster economic growth in ways that will provide a better life along with widening prosperity. We will incorporate labor and environmental concerns into U.S. trade negotiations, creating a healthy "network" between multilateral environmental agreements with the WTO, and use the International Labor Organization, trade preference programs, and trade talks to improve working conditions in conjunction with freer trade.

- *Enhance energy security.* We will strengthen our own energy security and the shared prosperity of the global economy by working with our allies, trading partners, and energy producers to expand the sources and types of global energy supplied, especially in the Western Hemisphere, Africa, Central Asia, and the Caspian region. We will also continue to work with our partners to develop cleaner and more energy efficient technologies.

Economic growth should be accompanied by global efforts to stabilize greenhouse gas concentrations associated with this growth, containing them at a level that prevents dangerous human interference with the global climate. Our overall objective is to reduce America's greenhouse gas emissions relative to the size of our economy, cutting such emissions per unit of economic activity by 18 percent over the next 10 years, by the year 2012. Our strategies for attaining this goal will be to:

- remain committed to the basic U.N. Framework Convention for international cooperation;

- obtain agreements with key industries to cut emissions of some of the most potent greenhouse gases and give transferable credits to companies that can show real cuts;

- develop improved standards for measuring and registering emission reductions;

- promote renewable energy production and clean coal technology, as well as nuclear power—which produces no greenhouse gas emissions, while also improving fuel economy for U.S. cars and trucks;

- increase spending on research and new conservation technologies, to a total of $4.5 billion—the largest sum being spent on climate change by any country in the world and a $700 million increase over last year's budget; and

- assist developing countries, especially the major greenhouse gas emitters such as China and India, so that they will have the tools and resources to join this effort and be able to grow along a cleaner and better path.

Chapter 7

EXPAND THE CIRCLE OF DEVELOPMENT BY OPENING SOCIETIES AND BUILDING THE INFRASTRUCTURE OF DEMOCRACY

> *"In World War II we fought to make the world safer, then worked to rebuild it. As we wage war today to keep the world safe from terror, we must also work to make the world a better place for all its citizens."*
>
> President Bush
> Washington, D.C. (Inter-American Development Bank)
> March 14, 2002

A world where some live in comfort and plenty, while half of the human race lives on less than $2 a day, is neither just nor stable. Including all of the world's poor in an expanding circle of development—and opportunity—is a moral imperative and one of the top priorities of U.S. international policy.

Decades of massive development assistance have failed to spur economic growth in the poorest countries. Worse, development aid has often served to prop up failed policies, relieving the pressure for reform and perpetuating misery. Results of aid are typically measured in dollars spent by donors, not in the rates of growth and poverty reduction achieved by recipients. These are the indicators of a failed strategy.

Working with other nations, the United States is confronting this failure. We forged a new consensus at the U.N. Conference on Financing for Development in Monterrey that the objectives of assistance—and the strategies to achieve those objectives—must change.

This Administration's goal is to help unleash the productive potential of individuals in all nations. Sustained growth and poverty reduction is impossible without the right national policies. Where governments have implemented real policy changes, we will provide significant new levels of assistance. The United States and other developed countries should set an ambitious and specific target: to double the size of the world's poorest economies within a decade.

The United States Government will pursue these major strategies to achieve this goal:

- *Provide resources to aid countries that have met the challenge of national reform.* We propose a 50 percent increase in the core development assistance given by the United States. While continuing our present programs, including humanitarian assistance based on need alone, these billions of new dollars will form a new Millennium Challenge Account for projects in countries whose governments rule justly, invest in their people, and encourage economic freedom. Governments must fight corruption, respect basic human rights, embrace the rule of law, invest in health care and education, follow responsible economic policies, and enable entrepreneurship. The Millennium Challenge Account will reward countries that have demonstrated real policy change and challenge those that have not to implement reforms.

- *Improve the effectiveness of the World Bank and other development banks in raising living standards.* The United States is committed to a comprehensive reform agenda for making the World Bank and the other multilateral development banks more effective in improving the lives of the world's poor.

- We have reversed the downward trend in U.S. contributions and proposed an 18 percent increase in the U.S. contributions to the International Development Association (IDA)—the World Bank's fund for the poorest countries—and the African Development Fund. The key to raising living standards and reducing poverty around the world is increasing productivity growth, especially in the poorest countries. We will continue to press the multilateral development banks to focus on activities that increase economic productivity, such as improvements in education, health, rule of law, and private sector development. Every project, every loan, every grant must be judged by how much it will increase productivity growth in developing countries.

- *Insist upon measurable results to ensure that development assistance is actually making a difference in the lives of the world's poor.* When it comes to economic development, what really matters is that more children are getting a better education, more people have access to health care and clean water, or more workers can find jobs to make a better future for their families. We have a moral obligation to measure the success of our development assistance by whether it is delivering results. For this reason, we will continue to demand that our own development assistance as well as assistance from the multilateral development banks has measurable goals and concrete benchmarks for achieving those goals. Thanks to U.S. leadership, the recent IDA replenishment agreement will establish a monitoring and evaluation system that measures recipient countries' progress. For the first time, donors can link a portion of their contributions to IDA to the achievement of actual development results, and part of the U.S. contribution is linked in this way. We will strive to make sure that the World Bank and other multilateral development banks build on this progress so that a focus on results is an integral part of everything that these institutions do.

- *Increase the amount of development assistance that is provided in the form of grants instead of loans.* Greater use of results-based grants is the best way to help poor countries make productive investments, particularly in the social sectors, without saddling them with ever-larger debt burdens. As a result of U.S. leadership, the recent IDA agreement provided for significant increases in grant funding for the poorest countries for education, HIV/AIDS, health, nutrition, water, sanitation, and other human needs. Our goal is to build on that progress by increasing the use of grants at the other multilateral development banks. We will also challenge universities, nonprofits, and the private sector to match government efforts by using grants to support development projects that show results.

- *Open societies to commerce and investment. Trade and investment are the real engines of economic growth.* Even if government aid increases, most money for development must come from trade, domestic capital, and foreign investment. An effective strategy must try to expand these flows as well. Free markets and free trade are key priorities of our national security strategy.

- *Secure public health.* The scale of the public health crisis in poor countries is enormous. In countries afflicted by epidemics and pandemics like HIV/AIDS, malaria, and tuberculosis, growth and development will be threatened until these scourges can be contained. Resources from the developed world are necessary but will be effective only with honest governance, which supports prevention programs and provides effective local infrastructure. The United States has strongly backed the new global fund for HIV/AIDS organized by U.N. Secretary General Kofi Annan and its focus on combining prevention with a broad strategy for treatment and care. The United States already contributes more than twice as much money to such efforts as the next largest donor. If the global fund demonstrates its promise, we will be ready to give even more.

- *Emphasize education.* Literacy and learning are the foundation of democracy and development. Only about 7 percent of World Bank resources are devoted to education. This proportion should grow. The United States will increase its own funding for education assistance by at least 20 percent with an emphasis on improving basic education and teacher training in Africa. The United States can also bring information technology to these societies, many of whose education systems have been devastated by HIV/AIDS.

- *Continue to aid agricultural development.* New technologies, including biotechnology, have enormous potential to improve crop yields in developing countries while using fewer pesticides and less water. Using sound science, the United States should help bring these benefits to the 800 million people, including 300 million children, who still suffer from hunger and malnutrition.

Chapter 8

DEVELOP AGENDAS FOR COOPERATIVE ACTION WITH THE OTHER MAIN CENTERS OF GLOBAL POWER

> *"We have our best chance since the rise of the nation-state in the 17th century to build a world where the great powers compete in peace instead of prepare for war."*
>
> President Bush
> West Point, New York
> June 1, 2002

America will implement its strategies by organizing coalitions—as broad as practicable— of states able and willing to promote a balance of power that favors freedom. Effective coalition leadership requires clear priorities, an appreciation of others' interests, and consistent consultations among partners with a spirit of humility.

There is little of lasting consequence that the United States can accomplish in the world without the sustained cooperation of its allies and friends in Canada and Europe. Europe is also the seat of two of the strongest and most able international institutions in the world: the North Atlantic Treaty Organization (NATO), which has, since its inception, been the fulcrum of transatlantic and inter-European security, and the European Union (EU), our partner in opening world trade.

The attacks of September 11 were also an attack on NATO, as NATO itself recognized when it invoked its Article V self-defense clause for the first time. NATO's core mission—collective defense of the transatlantic alliance of democracies —remains, but NATO must develop new structures and capabilities to carry out that mission under new circumstances. NATO must build a capability to field, at short notice, highly mobile, specially trained forces whenever they are needed to respond to a threat against any member of the alliance.

The alliance must be able to act wherever our interests are threatened, creating coalitions under NATO's own mandate, as well as contributing to mission-based coalitions. To achieve this, we must:

- expand NATO's membership to those democratic nations willing and able to share the burden of defending and advancing our common interests;

- ensure that the military forces of NATO nations have appropriate combat contributions to make in coalition warfare;

- develop planning processes to enable those contributions to become effective multinational fighting forces;

- take advantage of the technological opportunities and economies of scale in our defense spending to transform NATO military forces so that they dominate potential aggressors and diminish our vulnerabilities;

- streamline and increase the flexibility of command structures to meet new operational demands and the associated requirements of training, integrating, and experimenting with new force configurations; and

- maintain the ability to work and fight together as allies even as we take the necessary steps to transform and modernize our forces.

If NATO succeeds in enacting these changes, the rewards will be a partnership as central to the security and interests of its member states as was the case during the Cold War. We will sustain a common perspective on the threats to our societies and improve our ability to take common action in defense of our nations and their interests. At the same time, we welcome our European allies' efforts to forge a greater foreign policy and defense identity with the EU, and commit ourselves to close consultations to ensure that these developments work with NATO. We cannot afford to lose this opportunity to better prepare the family of transatlantic democracies for the challenges to come.

The attacks of September 11 energized America's Asian alliances. Australia invoked the ANZUS Treaty to declare the September 11 was an attack on Australia itself, following that historic decision with the dispatch of some of the world's finest combat forces for Operation Enduring Freedom. Japan and the Republic of Korea provided unprecedented levels of military logistical support within weeks of the terrorist attack. We have deepened cooperation on counterterrorism with our alliance partners in Thailand and the Philippines and received invaluable assistance from close friends like Singapore and New Zealand.

The war against terrorism has proven that America's alliances in Asia not only underpin regional peace and stability, but are flexible and ready to deal with new challenges. To enhance our Asian alliances and friendships, we will:

- look to Japan to continue forging a leading role in regional and global affairs based on our common interests, our common values, and our close defense and diplomatic cooperation;

- work with South Korea to maintain vigilance towards the North while preparing our alliance to make contributions to the broader stability of the region over the longer term;

- build on 50 years of U.S.-Australian alliance cooperation as we continue working together to resolve regional and global problems—as we have so many times from the Battle of the Coral Sea to Tora Bora;

- maintain forces in the region that reflect our commitments to our allies, our requirements, our technological advances, and the strategic environment; and

- build on stability provided by these alliances, as well as with institutions such as ASEAN and the Asia-Pacific Economic Cooperation forum, to develop a mix of regional and bilateral strategies to manage change in this dynamic region.

We are attentive to the possible renewal of old patterns of great power competition. Several potential great powers are now in the midst of internal transition—most importantly Russia, India, and China. In all three cases, recent developments have encouraged our hope that a truly global consensus about basic principles is slowly taking shape.

With Russia, we are already building a new strategic relationship based on a central reality of the twenty-first century: the United States and Russia are no longer strategic adversaries. The Moscow Treaty on Strategic Reductions is emblematic of this new reality and reflects a critical change in Russian thinking that promises to lead to productive, long-term relations with the Euro-Atlantic community and the United States. Russia's top leaders have a realistic assessment of their country's current weakness and the policies—internal and external—needed to reverse those weaknesses. They understand, increasingly, that Cold War approaches do not serve their national interests and that Russian and American strategic interests overlap in many areas.

United States policy seeks to use this turn in Russian thinking to refocus our relationship on emerging and potential common interests and challenges. We are broadening our already extensive cooperation in the global war on terrorism. We are facilitating Russia's entry into the World Trade Organization, without lowering standards for accession, to promote beneficial bilateral trade and investment relations. We have created the NATO-Russia Council with the goal of deepening security cooperation among Russia, our European allies, and ourselves. We will continue to bolster the independence and stability of the states of the former Soviet Union in the belief that a prosperous and stable neighborhood will reinforce Russia's growing commitment to integration into the Euro-Atlantic community.

At the same time, we are realistic about the differences that still divide us from Russia and about the time and effort it will take to build an enduring strategic partnership. Lingering distrust of our motives and policies by key Russian elites slows improvement in our relations. Russia's uneven commitment to the basic values of free-market democracy and dubious record in combating the proliferation of weapons of mass destruction remain matters of great concern. Russia's very weakness limits the opportunities for cooperation. Nevertheless, those opportunities are vastly greater now than in recent years—or even decades.

The United States has undertaken a transformation in its bilateral relationship with India based on a conviction that U.S. interests require a strong relationship with India. We are the two largest democracies, committed to political freedom protected by representative government. India is moving toward greater economic freedom as well. We have a common interest in the free flow of commerce, including through the vital sea lanes of the Indian Ocean. Finally, we share an interest in fighting terrorism and in creating a strategically stable Asia.

Differences remain, including over the development of India's nuclear and missile programs, and the pace of India's economic reforms. But while in the past these concerns may have dominated our thinking about India, today we start with a view of India as a growing world power with which we have common strategic interests. Through a strong partnership with India, we can best address any differences and shape a dynamic future.

The United States relationship with China is an important part of our strategy to promote a stable, peaceful, and prosperous Asia-Pacific region. We welcome the emergence of a strong, peaceful, and prosperous China. The democratic development of China is crucial to that future. Yet, a quarter century after beginning the process of shedding the worst features of the Communist legacy, China's leaders have not yet made the next series of fundamental choices about the character of their state. In pursuing advanced military capabilities that can threaten its neighbors in the Asia-Pacific region, China is following an outdated path that, in the end, will hamper its own pursuit of national greatness. In time, China will find that social and political freedom is the only source of that greatness.

The United States seeks a constructive relationship with a changing China. We already cooperate well where our interests overlap, including the current war on terrorism and in promoting stability on the Korean peninsula. Likewise, we have coordinated on the future of Afghanistan and have initiated a comprehensive dialogue on counterterrorism and similar transitional concerns. Shared health and environmental threats, such as the spread of HIV/AIDS, challenge us to promote jointly the welfare of our citizens.

Addressing these transnational threats will challenge China to become more open with information, promote the development of civil society, and enhance individual human rights. China has begun to take the road to political openness, permitting many personal freedoms and conducting village-level elections, yet remains strongly committed to national one-party rule by the Communist Party. To make that nation truly accountable to its citizen's needs and aspirations, however, much work remains to be done. Only by allowing the Chinese people to think, assemble, and worship freely can China reach its full potential.

Our important trade relationship will benefit from China's entry into the World Trade Organization, which will create more export opportunities and ultimately more jobs for American farmers, workers, and companies. China is our fourth largest trading partner, with over $100 billion in annual two-way trade. The power of market principles and the WTO's requirements for transparency and accountability will advance openness and the rule of law in China to help establish basic protections for commerce and for citizens. There are, however, other areas in which we have profound disagreements. Our commitment to the self-defense of Taiwan under the Taiwan Relations Act is one. Human rights is another. We expect China to adhere to its nonproliferation commitments. We will work to narrow differences where they exist, but not allow them to preclude cooperation where we agree.

The events of September 11, 2001, fundamentally changed the context for relations between the United States and other main centers of global power, and opened vast, new opportunities. With our long-standing allies in Europe and Asia, and with leaders in Russia, India, and China, we must develop active agendas of cooperation lest these relationships become routine and unproductive.

Every agency of the United States Government shares the challenge. We can build fruitful habits of consultation, quiet argument, sober analysis, and common action. In the long-term, these are the practices that will sustain the supremacy of our common principles and keep open the path of progress.

Chapter 9

TRANSFORM AMERICA'S NATIONAL SECURITY INSTITUTIONS TO MEET THE CHALLENGES AND OPPORTUNITIES OF THE TWENTY-FIRST CENTURY

> *"Terrorists attacked a symbol of American prosperity. They did not touch its source. America is successful because of the hard work, creativity, and enterprise of our people."*
>
> President Bush
> Washington, D.C. (Joint Session of Congress)
> September 20, 2001

The major institutions of American national security were designed in a different era to meet different requirements. All of them must be transformed.

It is time to reaffirm the essential role of American military strength. We must build and maintain our defenses beyond challenge. Our military's highest priority is to defend the United States. To do so effectively, our military must:

- assure our allies and friends;
- dissuade future military competition;
- deter threats against U.S. interests, allies, and friends; and
- decisively defeat any adversary if deterrence fails.

The unparalleled strength of the United States armed forces, and their forward presence, have maintained the peace in some of the world's most strategically vital regions. However, the threats and enemies we must confront have changed, and so must our forces. A military structured to deter massive Cold War-era armies must be transformed to focus more on how an adversary might fight rather than where and when a war might occur. We will channel our energies to overcome a host of operational challenges.

The presence of American forces overseas is one of the most profound symbols of the U.S. commitments to allies and friends. Through our willingness to use force in our own defense and in defense of others, the United States demonstrates its resolve to maintain a balance of power that favors freedom. To contend with uncertainty and to meet the many security challenges we face, the United States will require bases and stations within and beyond Western Europe and Northeast Asia, as well as temporary access arrangements for the long-distance deployment of U.S. forces.

Before the war in Afghanistan, that area was low on the list of major planning contingencies. Yet, in a very short time, we had to operate across the length and breadth of that remote nation, using every branch of the armed forces. We must prepare for more such deployments by developing assets such as advanced remote sensing, long-range precision strike capabilities, and transformed maneuver and expeditionary forces. This broad portfolio of military capabilities must also include the ability to defend the homeland, conduct information operations, ensure U.S. access to distant theaters, and protect critical U.S. infrastructure and assets in outer space.

Innovation within the armed forces will rest on experimentation with new approaches to warfare, strengthening joint operations, exploiting U.S. intelligence advantages, and taking full advantage of science and technology. We must also transform the way the Department of Defense is run, especially in financial management and recruitment and retention. Finally, while maintaining near-term readiness and the ability to fight the war on terrorism, the goal must be to provide the President with a wider range of military options to discourage aggression or any form of coercion against the United States, our allies, and our friends.

We know from history that deterrence can fail; and we know from experience that some enemies cannot be deterred. The United States must and will maintain the capability to defeat any attempt by an enemy—whether a state or non-state actor—to impose its will on the United States, our allies, or our friends. We will maintain the forces sufficient to support our obligations, and to defend freedom. Our forces will be strong enough to dissuade potential adversaries from pursuing a military build-up in hopes of surpassing, or equaling, the power of the United States.

Intelligence—and how we use it—is our first line of defense against terrorists and the threat posed by hostile states. Designed around the priority of gathering enormous information about a massive, fixed object—the Soviet bloc—the intelligence community is coping with the challenge of following a far more complex and elusive set of targets.

We must transform our intelligence capabilities and build new ones to keep pace with the nature of these threats. Intelligence must be appropriately integrated with our defense and law enforcement systems and coordinated with our allies and friends. We need to protect the capabilities we have so that we do not arm our enemies with the knowledge of how best to surprise us. Those who would harm us also seek the benefit of surprise to limit our prevention and response options and to maximize injury.

We must strengthen intelligence warning and analysis to provide integrated threat assessments for national and homeland security. Since the threats inspired by foreign governments and groups may be conducted inside the United States, we must also ensure the proper fusion of information between intelligence and law enforcement.

Initiatives in this area will include:

- strengthening the authority of the Director of Central Intelligence to lead the development and actions of the Nation's foreign intelligence capabilities;

- establishing a new framework for intelligence warning that provides seamless and integrated warning across the spectrum of threats facing the nation and our allies;

- continuing to develop new methods of collecting information to sustain our intelligence advantage;

- investing in future capabilities while working to protect them through a more vigorous effort to prevent the compromise of intelligence capabilities; and

- collecting intelligence against the terrorist danger across the government with allsource analysis.

As the United States Government relies on the armed forces to defend America's interests, it must rely on diplomacy to interact with other nations.

We will ensure that the Department of State receives funding sufficient to ensure the success of American diplomacy. The State Department takes the lead in managing our bilateral relationships with other governments. And in this new era, its people and institutions must be able to interact equally adroitly with non-governmental organizations and international institutions. Officials trained mainly in international politics must also extend their reach to understand complex issues of domestic governance around the world, including public health, education, law enforcement, the judiciary, and public diplomacy.

Our diplomats serve at the front line of complex negotiations, civil wars, and other humanitarian catastrophes. As humanitarian relief requirements are better understood, we must also be able to help build police forces, court systems, and legal codes, local and provincial government institutions, and electoral systems. Effective international cooperation is needed to accomplish these goals, backed by American readiness to play our part.

Just as our diplomatic institutions must adapt so that we can reach out to others, we also need a different and more comprehensive approach to public information efforts that can help people around the world learn about and understand America. The war on terrorism is not a clash of civilizations. It does, however, reveal the clash inside a civilization, a battle for the future of the Muslim world. This is a struggle of ideas and this is an area where America must excel.

We will take the actions necessary to ensure that our efforts to meet our global security commitments and protect Americans are not impaired by the potential for investigations, inquiry, or prosecution by the International Criminal Court (ICC), whose jurisdiction does not extend to Americans and which we do not accept. We will work together with other nations to avoid complications in our military operations and cooperation, through such mechanisms as multilateral and bilateral agreements that will protect U.S. nationals from the ICC. We will implement fully the American Service members Protection Act, whose provisions are intended to ensure and enhance the protection of U.S. personnel and officials.

We will make hard choices in the coming year and beyond to ensure the right level and allocation of government spending on national security. The United States Government must strengthen its defenses to win this war. At home, our most important priority is to protect the homeland for the American people.

Today, the distinction between domestic and foreign affairs is diminishing. In a globalized world, events beyond America's borders have a greater impact inside them. Our society must be open to people, ideas, and goods from across the globe. The characteristics we most cherish—our freedom, our cities, our systems of movement, and modern life—are vulnerable to terrorism. This vulnerability will persist long after we bring to justice those responsible for the September 11 attacks. As time passes, individuals may gain access to means of destruction that until now could be wielded only by armies, fleets, and squadrons. This is a new condition of life. We will adjust to it and thrive—in spite of it.

In exercising our leadership, we will respect the values, judgment, and interests of our friends and partners. Still, we will be prepared to act apart when our interests and unique responsibilities require. When we disagree on particulars, we will explain forthrightly the grounds for our concerns and strive to forge viable alternatives. We will not allow such disagreements to obscure our determination to secure together, with our allies and our friends, our shared fundamental interests and values.

Ultimately, the foundation of American strength is at home. It is in the skills of our people, the dynamism of our economy, and the resilience of our institutions. A diverse, modern society has inherent, ambitious, entrepreneurial energy. Our strength comes from what we do with that energy. That is where our national security begins.

Chapter 10

STRENGTHENING INTELLIGENCE TO BETTER PROTECT AMERICA

TODAY'S PRESIDENTIAL ACTION

In his State of the Union Address, President Bush announced a new initiative to better protect America by continuing to close the "seam" between analysis of foreign and domestic intelligence on terrorism. The President announced that he has instructed the Director of Central Intelligence, the Director of the FBI, working with the Attorney General, and the Secretaries of Homeland Security and Defense to develop the Nation's first unified Terrorist Threat Integration Center. This new center will merge and analyze terrorist-related information collected domestically and abroad in order to form the most comprehensive possible threat picture. Since September 11, 2001, our government has been working together and sharing information like never before. The creation of the Terrorist Threat Integration Center is the next phase in the dramatic enhancement of the government's counterterrorism effort. The President has now directed his senior advisors to take the next step in ensuring that intelligence information from all sources is shared, integrated, and analyzed seamlessly -- and then acted upon quickly. The Administration will ensure that this program is carried out consistently with the rights of Americans.

The New Terrorist Threat Integration Center

Elements of the Department of Homeland Security, the FBI's Counterterrorism Division, the DCI's Counterterrorist Center, and the Department of Defense will form a Terrorist Threat Integration Center to fuse and analyze all-source information related to terrorism. The Terrorist Threat Integration Center will continue to close the "seam" between analysis of foreign and domestic intelligence on terrorism. Specifically, it will:

- Optimize use of terrorist threat-related information, expertise, and capabilities to conduct threat analysis and inform collection strategies.

- Create a structure that ensures information sharing across agency lines.

- Integrate terrorist-related information collected domestically and abroad in order to form the most comprehensive possible threat picture.

- Be responsible and accountable for providing terrorist threat assessments for our national leadership.

The Terrorist Threat Integration Center will be headed by a senior U.S. Government official, who will report to the Director of Central Intelligence. This individual will be appointed by the Director of Central Intelligence, in consultation with the Director of the FBI and the Attorney General, the Secretary of Defense, and the Secretary of Homeland Security. The Terrorist Threat Integration Center will play a lead role in overseeing a national counterterrorism tasking and requirements system and for maintaining shared databases. The Terrorist Threat Integration Center will also maintain an up-to-date database of known and suspected terrorists that will be accessible to federal and non-federal officials and entities, as appropriate. In order to carry out its responsibilities effectively, the Terrorist Threat Integration Center will have access to all intelligence information—from raw reports to finished analytic assessments—available to the U.S. Government. A senior multiagency team will finalize the details, design, and implementation strategy for the stand-up of the Terrorist Threat Integration Center.

TRANSFORMING THE FEDERAL BUREAU OF INVESTIGATION

Immediately after September 11, the President directed the FBI and the Attorney General to make preventing future terrorist attacks against the homeland their top priority – and they have responded. The FBI has:

- Disrupted terrorist plots on U.S. soil.

- Established 66 Joint Terrorism Task Forces across America, with full participation from, and enhanced communications with, multiple federal, state, and local agencies.

- Created a National Joint Terrorism Task Force at FBI Headquarters.

- Established a 24-7 Counterterrorism Watch center.

- Created new counterterrorism "Flying Squads" to deploy into the field at a moment's notice.

- Created Intelligence Reports Offices to facilitate the vital flow of information.

- Trained new analysts for the Counterterrorism Division, using a curriculum developed with assistance from the CIA.

The FBI is establishing an intelligence program to ensure that the collection and dissemination of intelligence is given the same institutional priority as the collection of evidence for prosecution. A new Executive Assistant Director for Intelligence will have direct authority and responsibility for the FBI's national intelligence program. The FBI is establishing intelligence units in all of its Field Offices. The FBI is implementing a revolutionary new data management system to ensure that it shares all the FBI's terrorism-related information internally and with the CIA, the Department of Homeland Security, and other appropriate agencies. Last year, by enacting the USA PATRIOT Act, the President and Congress took an important step to enhance the ability of the FBI and other law enforcement agencies to investigate and prosecute terrorism, and to share information with other government agencies.

ENHANCING CIA'S COUNTERTERRORISM CAPABILITIES

Counterterrorism is a long-standing priority of the CIA and the CIA has been pivotal to the major successes in America's War on Terror. The CIA has:

- Disrupted dozens of planned terrorist attacks around the world.

- Continued to expand our insight into terrorist organizations and plans.

- Greatly enhanced its working relationships with foreign partners.

Since September 11, 2001, the Director of Central Intelligence has dramatically redeployed analysts and operatives against the terrorist target. He has: Doubled the size of the Counterterrorist Center. Quadrupled the number of personnel engaged in counterterrorism analysis. Detailed 25 experienced analysts to work side by side with their counterparts at FBI. The DCI created the position of Associate Director of Central Intelligence for Homeland Security to ensure timely, effective and secure flow of intelligence to agencies engaged in Homeland Security.

A KEY ROLE FOR THE DEPARTMENT OF HOMELAND SECURITY

The Department of Homeland Security will add critical new capabilities in the area of information analysis and infrastructure protection. The Department's Information Analysis and Infrastructure Protection Directorate will:

- Perform comprehensive vulnerability assessments of the Nation's critical infrastructure and key assets.

- Receive and analyze terrorism-related information from the Terrorism Threat Integration Center, as well as open sources, the public, private industry, state and local law enforcement, and the entire federal family.

- Map the threats against our vulnerabilities, in order to develop a comprehensive picture of the terrorist threat and our ability to withstand it.

- Take and facilitate action to protect against identified threats, remedy vulnerabilities, and preempt and disrupt terrorist threats, as consistent with the operational authorities of the Department's constituent agencies.

- Set national priorities for infrastructure protection, strategically designed to maximize the return on the investment

- Take a lead role in issuing warnings, threat advisories, and recommended response measures to America's public safety agencies, elected officials, industry, and the public.

The Department will be a full partner in the Terrorist Threat Integration Center. The Terrorist Threat Integration Center will help the Department perform its critical missions. It will provide the Department with a full and comprehensive picture of the terrorist threat that will inform the actions of the Department. Some of the Department's functions are expected to be performed at the new facility housing the Terrorist Threat Integration Center.

The integration of elements of the Department into the Terrorist Threat Integration Center will ensure an unimpeded two-way flow of terrorist threat information. The Department of Homeland Security, working hand in hand with the FBI, will be responsible for ensuring that threat information, including information produced by the Center, is disseminated quickly to the public, private industry, and state and local governments as appropriate.

CONTRIBUTIONS OF THE DEPARTMENT OF DEFENSE

The Department of Defense has been a key player in the global war on terrorism, including prosecuting the war on terrorism overseas. Intelligence elements of the Department, including the National Security Agency, the

Defense Intelligence Agency, the National Imagery and Mapping Agency, continue to make crucial contributions to our terrorism intelligence collection overseas. Appropriate DOD intelligence elements will participate fully in the TTIC, providing information, receiving information, and contributing to analytic efforts, under their own current authorities. DOD will have no new operational authority or responsibility under the President's announced program. The TTIC does not involve new activities by DOD; rather, it seeks to maximize and "fuse" the efforts of all of our counterterrorism intelligence efforts, as has been called for by many experts on both sides of the aisle.

PART II.
ANALYSES OF PREEMPTIVE FORCE

Chapter 11

RESPONSE TO TERRORISM: LEGAL ASPECTS OF THE USE OF MILITARY FORCE

David M. Ackerman

SUMMARY

The terrorist attack of September 11, 2001, has precipitated widespread calls for the use of military force in response. Under U.S. and international law a variety of legal considerations attach to such use. This report briefly summarizes several salient aspects.

Legal considerations concerning the use of force under U.S. and international law include the following:

(1) ACTS OF WAR

War has been defined as "a condition of armed hostility between States"[1] or, in Grotius' terms, as the "state or condition of governments contending by force."[2] An act of war, thus, involves the threat or use of force of some kind by one state against another. But whether a particular threat or

---

[1] Hyde, Charles Cheney, International Law Chiefly as Interpreted and Applied by the United States, Vol. 3 (1945), at 1686.

[2] Id. n. 1. Grotius was one of the original theorists of international law.

use of force constitutes an act of war depends heavily on how the parties choose to characterize it. For the United States acts of foreign governments that have been deemed to constitute acts of war have ranged from the impressment of U.S. seamen into service in the British navy to failure to honor U.S. neutrality in conflicts between other states to Japan's attack on Pearl Harbor.

(2) Declaration of War

Article I, § 8, of the Constitution confers on Congress the power to "declare War." That power comprehends not only the enactment of formal declarations of war but also the authorization of uses of military force which are not intended to rise to the level of a war. Congress has enacted eleven formal declarations of war relating to five different conflicts – the War of 1812, the Mexican-American War in 1846, the Spanish-American War in 1898, World War I, and World War II. It has also enacted numerous authorizations for the use of military force that have **not** constituted declarations of war, such as the Tonkin Gulf Resolution of 1964[3] and the 1991 "Authorization for Use of Military Force Against Iraq Resolution."[4] One domestic effect of a declaration of war is that it brings into effect a number of statutes that confer discretionary authority on the President.

(3) President's Authority to Use Military Force

Article II, § 1, of the Constitution vests the "executive Power" of the government in the President. Article II, § 2, states that the President "shall be Commander in Chief of the Army and Navy of the United States, and of the Militia of the several States, when called into the actual Service of the United States." These clauses clearly empower the President to direct the conduct of a war or other military engagement authorized by Congress. But it has often been argued that these clauses, as well as the inherent authority that accrues to the President by virtue of the existence of the United States as a sovereign nation, empower the President to initiate the use of force even absent Congressional authorization. Others contend otherwise. But however

---

[3] P.L. 88-408 (August 10, 1964).
[4] P.L. 102-1 (Jan. 14, 1991).

that debate is resolved in a given situation, virtually all commentators concur that the President has the constitutional authority to defend the United States from sudden attack even absent Congressional authorization. Whether that authority is wholly defensive or can also involve the use of offensive force in a given situation, however, has been the subject of dispute between Congress and the President.

(4) WAR POWERS RESOLUTION

To protect its constitutional role regarding the use of military force, Congress in 1973 enacted the "War Powers Resolution" (WPR)[5] over President Nixon's veto. That enactment specifically recognizes the President's authority to use military force in "a national emergency created by attack upon the United States, its territories or possessions, or its armed forces." But it requires the President to "consult with Congress ... in every possible instance" prior to employing force and to submit a report to Congress on any such instance. Most critically, it requires the President to terminate U.S. involvement in hostilities within 60-90 days unless Congress has enacted a declaration of war or a specific authorization for such involvement, has extended the 60-day period by statute, or is unable to meet because of an armed attack on the United States. Every President since Nixon has regarded the WPR as an unconstitutional intrusion on his prerogatives regarding the use of force.

(5) UNITED NATIONS CHARTER

The UN Charter was adopted in part "to save succeeding generations from the scourge of war" (Preamble). As a consequence, it requires its Members to "refrain in their international relations from the threat or use of force against the territorial integrity or political independence of any State, or in any other manner inconsistent with the Purposes of the United Nations" (Article 2(4)); and it provides for collective action under the auspices of the Security Council to maintain or restore international peace and security (Chapter VII). However, the Charter also recognizes a right of self-defense. Article 51 provides that "[n]othing in the present Charter shall impair the inherent right of individual or collective self-defence if an armed attack

---

[5] P.L. 93-148 (Nov. 7, 1973); 50 U.S.C. 1541 et seq.

occurs against a Member of the United Nations, until the Security Council has taken measures necessary to maintain international peace and security...."

Chapter 12

U.S. USE OF PREEMPTIVE MILITARY FORCE

Richard F. Grimmett

SUMMARY

This chapter reviews the historical record regarding the uses of U.S. military force in a "preemptive" manner, an issue that has emerged due to the possible use of U.S. military force against Iraq. It examines and comments on military actions taken by the United States that could be reasonably interpreted as "preemptive" in nature. For purposes of this analysis we consider a "preemptive" use of military force to be the taking of military action by the United States against another nation so as to prevent or mitigate a presumed *military* attack or use of force by that nation against the United States. We *do not* deem the deployment of U.S. military forces in support of U.S. foreign policy, without their engaging in combat, to be a "preemptive" use of military force. This review includes all noteworthy uses of military force by the United States since the establishment of the Republic.

BACKGROUND

In recent months the question of the possible use of "preemptive" military force by the United States to defend its security has been raised by President Bush and members of his Administration, including possible use of such force against Iraq.[1] This analysis reviews the historical record regarding the uses of U.S. military force in a "preemptive" manner. It examines and comments on military actions taken by the United States that could be reasonably interpreted as "preemptive" in nature. For purposes of this analysis we consider a "preemptive" use of military force to be the taking of military action by the United States against another nation so as to prevent or mitigate a presumed *military* attack or use of force by that nation against the United States. We do not deem the deployment of U.S. military forces in support of U.S. foreign policy, without their engaging in combat, to be a "preemptive" use of military force.[2] The discussion below is based upon our review of all noteworthy uses of military force by the United States since establishment of the Republic.

HISTORICAL OVERVIEW

The historical record indicates that the United States has never, to date, engaged in a "preemptive" military attack against another nation. Nor has the United States ever attacked another nation militarily prior to its first having been attacked or prior to U.S. citizens or interests first having been attacked, with the singular exception of the Spanish-American War. The Spanish-American War is unique in that the principal goal of United States military action was to compel Spain to grant Cuba its political independence. An act of Congress passed just prior to the U.S. declaration of war against Spain explicitly declared Cuba to be independent of Spain, demanded that Spain withdraw its military forces from the island, and authorized the President to use U.S. military force to achieve these ends.[3] Spain rejected these demands,

---

[1] See speeches of President George W. Bush at West Point on June 1, 2002 at[http://www.whitehouse.gov/news/releases/2002/06/20020601-3.html]; and the President'sUnited Nations. speech of September 12, 2002 at[http://www.whitehouse.govnews/releases/2002/09/20020912-1.html]; Washington Post, June2, 2002, p. A1; Washington Post, September 13, 2002, p.A1.

[2] It is important to note here the historic and traditional view of the United States government onwhat constitutes the legitimate use of preemptive military force in accordance with international law. This view was best articulated by then Secretary of State, Daniel Webster, in 1842, in diplomatic correspondence with the British Government. Webster stated that it was an act of self-defense permitting an intrusion into the territory of another state only in those "cases in which the necessity of that self-defense is instant, overwhelming, and leaving no choice of means andno moment for deliberation." See letter from Secretary of State Daniel Webster to Lord Ashburton of August 6, 1842, reprinted in Moore, John Bassett, A Digest of International Law, Vol. II (1906), p. 412. For a detailed discussion of international law and preemptive use of military force see CRS Report RS21314,International Law and the Preemptive Use of Force Against Iraq, by David M. Ackerman.

[3] Joint Resolution of April 20, 1898, [Res. 24] 30 Stat. 738.

and an exchange of declarations of war by both countries soon followed.[4] Although U.S. military actions against Spain were based on special U.S. foreign policy considerations, they occurred after war was formally declared, and cannot be fairly characterized as "preemptive" in nature. Various instances of the use of force are discussed below that could, using a less stringent definition, be argued by some as historic examples of "preemption" by the United States. The final case, the Cuban Missile crisis of 1962, represents a threat situation which some may argue had elements more parallel to those presented by Iraq today - but it was resolved without a "preemptive" military attack by the United States. The circumstances surrounding the origins of the Mexican War are somewhat controversial in nature - but the term "preemptive" attack by the United States does not apply to this conflict. During, and immediately following the First World War, the United States, as part of allied military operations, sent military forces into parts of Russia to protect its interests, and to render limited aid to anti-Bolshevik forces during the Russian civil war. In major military actions since the Second World War, the President has either obtained congressional authorization for use of military force against other nations, in advance of using it, or has directed military actions abroad on his own initiative in support of multinational operations such as those of the United Nations or of mutual security arrangements like the North Atlantic Treaty Organization (NATO). Examples of these actions include participation in the Korean War, the 1990-1991 Persian Gulf War, and the Bosnian and Kosovo operations in the 1990s. Yet in all of these varied instances of the use of military force by the United States, such military action was a "response," after the fact, and was not "preemptive" in nature.

CENTRAL AMERICAN AND CARIBBEAN INTERVENTIONS

This is not to say that the United States has not used its military to intervene in other nations in support of its foreign policy interests. However,

---

[4] There was no direct military attack by Spain against the United States prior to the exchange ofdeclarations of war by the nations, and initiation of hostilities by the United States in 1898. SeeDeclarations of War and Authorizations for the Use of Military Force: Historical Backgroundand Legal Implications. CRS Report RL31133, by David M. Ackerman and Richard F.Grimmett. A notable event, the sinking of the U.S.S. Maine in Havana harbor, provided anadditional argument for war against Spain for those advocating it in the United States. The actual cause of the sinking of the U.S.S. Maine in Havana harbor, even today, has not been definitively established. More recent scholarship argues that it was most likely not due to an external attack on the ship, such as the use of a mine by an outside party, but due to an internal explosion.

U.S. military interventions, particularly a number of unilateral uses of force in the Central America and Caribbean areas throughout the 20th century were not "preemptive" in nature. What led the United States to intervene militarily in nations in these areas was not the view that the individual nations were likely to attack the United States militarily. Rather, these U.S. military interventions were grounded in the view that they would support the Monroe Doctrine, which opposed interference in the Western hemisphere by outside nations. U.S. policy was driven by the belief that if stable governments existed in Caribbean states and Central America, then it was less likely that foreign countries would attempt to protect their nationals or their economic interests through their use of military force against one or more of these nations.

Consequently, the United States, in the early part of the 20thcentury, established through treaties with the Dominican Republic (in 1907)[5] and with Haiti (in 1915)[6], the right for the United States to collect and disperse customs income received by these nations, as well as the right to protect the Receiver General of customs and his assistants in the performance of his duties. This effectively created U.S. protectorates for these countries until these arrangements were terminated during the Administration of President Franklin D. Roosevelt. Intermittent domestic insurrections against the national governments in both countries led the U.S. to utilize American military forces to restore order in Haiti from 1915-1934 and in the Dominican Republic from 1916-1924. But the purpose of these interventions, buttressed by the treaties with the United States, was tohelp maintain or restore political stability, and thus eliminate the potential for foreign military intervention in contravention of the principles of the Monroe Doctrine.

Similar concerns about foreign intervention in a politically unstable Nicaragua led the United States in 1912 to accept the request of its then President Adolfo Diaz to intervene militarily to restore political order there. Through the Bryan-Chamorro treaty with Nicaragua in 1914, the United States obtained the right to protect the Panama Canal, and its proprietary rights to any future canal through Nicaragua as well as islands leased from Nicaragua for use as military installations. This treaty also granted to the United States the right to take any measure needed to carry out the treaty's purposes.[7] This treaty had the effect of making Nicaragua a quasi-protectorate of the United States. Since political turmoil in the country might threaten the Panama Canal or U.S. proprietary rights to build another canal, the U.S. employed that rationale to justify the intervention and long-term

---

[5] 7 UST 196.
[6] 8 UST 660.
[7] 10 UST 379.

presence of American military forces in Nicaragua to maintain political stability in the country. U.S. military forces were permanently withdrawn from Nicaragua in 1933. Apart from the above cases, U.S. military interventions in the Dominican Republic in 1965, Grenada in 1983, and in Panama in 1989 were based upon concerns that U.S. citizens or other U.S. interests were being harmed by the political instability in these countries at the time U.S. intervention occurred. While U.S. military interventions in Central America and Caribbean nations were controversial, after reviewing the context in which they occurred, it is fair to say that none of them involved the use of "preemptive" military force by the United States.[8]

COVERT ACTION

Although the use of "preemptive" force by the United States is generally associated with the overt use of U.S. military forces, it is important to note that the United States has also utilized "covert action" by U.S. government personnel in efforts to influence political and military outcomes in other nations. The public record indicates that the United States has used this form of intervention to prevent some groups or political figures from gaining or maintaining political power to the detriment of U.S. interests and those of friendly nations. For example, the use of "covert action" was widely reported to have been successfully employed to effect changes in the governments of Iran in 1953, and in Guatemala in 1954. Its use failed in the case of Cuba in 1961. The general approach in the use of a "covert action" is reportedly to support local political and military/paramilitary forces in gaining or maintaining political control in a nation, so that U.S. or its allies interests will not be threatened. None of these activities has reportedly involved significant numbers of U.S. military forces because by their very nature "covert actions" are efforts to advance an outcome without drawing direct attention to the United States in the process of doing so.[9] Such previous clandestine operations by U.S. personnel could arguably have constituted

---

[8] For an excellent background discussion of U.S. policy toward the Caribbean and Central American nations during the first half of the 20thcentury see: Samuel Flagg Bemis, A Diplomatic History of the United States. New York. Holt, Rinehart and Winston, Inc. 1965, pp. 519-538.For a detailed historical study that provides valuable insights and commentary on U.S. actions taken toward Caribbean and Central American countries see chapters 9, 11, and 12 in Samuel Flagg Bemis, The Latin American Policy of the United States. New York. Harcourt, Brace &World , 1943. [reprinted in paperback in New York, by W. W. Norton & Company, Inc., 1967].

[9] Section 503(e) of the National Security Act of 1947, as amended, defines covert action as "An activity or activities of the United States Government to influence political, economic or military conditions abroad, where it is intended that the role of the United States Government will not be apparent or acknowledged publicly."

efforts at "preemptive" action to forestall unwanted political or military developments in other nations. But given their presumptive limited scale compared to those of major conventional military operations, it seems more appropriate to view U.S. "covert actions" as adjuncts to more extensive U.S. military actions. As such, prior U.S. "covert actions" do not appear to be true case examples of the use of "preemptive" military force by the United States.

CUBAN MISSILE CRISIS OF 1962

The one significant, well documented, case of note, where "preemptive" military action was seriously contemplated by the United States, but ultimately not used, was the Cuban missile crisis of October 1962. When the United States learned from spy-plane photographs that the Soviet Union was secretly introducing nuclear-capable, intermediate-range ballistic missiles into Cuba, missiles that could threaten a large portion of the Eastern United States, President John F. Kennedy had to determine if the prudent course of action was to use U.S. military air strikes in an effort to destroy the missile sites before they became operational, and before the Soviets or the Cubans became aware that the U.S. knew they were being installed. While the military "preemption" option was considered, after extensive debate among his advisors on the implications of such an action, President Kennedy undertook a measured but firm approach to the crisis that utilized a U.S. military "quarantine" of the island of Cuba to prevent further shipments from the Soviet Union of military supplies and material for the existing missile sites, while a diplomatic solution was aggressively pursued. This approach was successful, and the crisis was peacefully resolved.[10]

---

[10] For detailed background regarding the issues surrounding the possible use of "preemptive" military force against the Soviet missile sites being established in Cuba, and the deliberative process engaged in by President Kennedy and his key advisors, see the published transcripts of tape recordings made during their White House meetings in The Kennedy Tapes: Inside the White House during the Cuban Missile Crisis. Ernest R. May and Philip D. Zelikow (eds.). Cambridge, Massachusetts. Harvard University Press, 1997.

Chapter 11

INTERNATIONAL LAW AND THE PREEMPTIVE USE OF FORCE AGAINST IRAQ

David M. Ackerman

SUMMARY

In his speech to the United Nations on September 12, 2002, President Bush described the regime of Saddam Hussein in Iraq as "a grave and gathering danger," detailed that regime's persistent efforts to acquire weapons of mass destruction and its persistent defiance of numerous Security Council resolutions requiring Iraq to disarm, and raised the specter of an "outlaw regime" providing such weapons to terrorists. The President left little doubt that, with or without UN support, the United States would act to force Iraq to disarm and otherwise abide by its past commitments, and that military force might well be used to accomplish that objective. One issue raised by that policy is the legality of the preemptive use of force under international law. This chapter examines that issue as developed in customary international law and under the United Nations Charter. It will be updated as events warrant.

Preemptive Military Attacks Under Customary International Law

Until recent decades customary international law deemed the right to use force and even to go to war to be an essential attribute of every state. As one scholar summarized:

> It always lies within the power of a State to endeavor to obtain redress for wrongs, or to gain political or other advantages over another, not merely by the employment of force, but also by direct recourse to war.[1]

Within that framework customary international law also consistently recognized self-defense as a legitimate basis for the use of force:

> An act of self-defense is that form of self-protection which is directed against an aggressor or contemplated aggressor. No act can be so described which is not occasioned by attack or fear of attack. When acts of self-preservation on the part of a State are strictly acts of self-defense, they are permitted by the law of nations, and are justified on principle, even though they may conflict with the ... rights of other states.[2]

Moreover, the recognized right of a state to use force for purposes of self-defense traditionally included the preemptive use of force, i.e., the use of force in anticipation of an attack. Hugo Grotius, the father of international law, stated in the seventeenth century that "[i]t be lawful to kill him who is preparing to kill."[3] Emmerich de Vattel a century later similarly asserted:

> The safest plan is to prevent evil, where that is possible. A Nation has the right to resist the injury another seeks to inflict upon it, and to use force ... against the aggressor. It may even anticipate the other's design, being careful, however, not to act upon vague and doubtful suspicions, lest it should run the risk of becoming itself the aggressor.[4]

The classic formulation of the right of preemptive attack was given by Secretary of State Daniel Webster in connection with the famous Caroline

---

[1] Hyde, Charles Cheney, International Law Chiefly As Interpreted and Applied by the United States, Vol. 3 (1945), at 1686.
[2] Id. Vol. 1, at 237.
[3] Grotius, Hugo, The Law of War and Peace, at 1625.
[4] de Vattel, Emmerich, The Law of Nations, Vol. IV, at 3.

incident. In 1837 British troops under the cover of night attacked and sank an American ship, the Caroline, in U.S. waters because the ship was being used to provide supplies to insurrectionists against British rule in Canada headquartered on an island on the Canadian side of the Niagara River. The U.S. immediately protested this "extraordinary outrage" and demanded an apology and reparations. The dispute dragged on for several years before the British conceded that they ought to have immediately offered "some explanation and apology." But in the course of the diplomatic exchanges Secretary of State Daniel Webster articulated the two conditions essential to the legitimacy of the preemptive use of force under customary international law. In one note he asserted that an intrusion into the territory of another state can be justified as an act of self-defense only in those "cases in which the necessity of that self-defense is instant, overwhelming, and leaving no choice of means and no moment for deliberation."[5] In another note he asserted that the force used in such circumstances has to be proportional to the threat:

> It will be for [Her Majesty's Government] to show, also, that the local authorities of Canada, even supposing the necessity of the moment authorized them to enter the territories of the United States at all, did nothing unreasonable or excessive; since the act, justified by the necessity of self-defence, must be limited by that necessity, and kept clearly within it.[6]

Both elements – necessity and proportionality – have been deemed essential to legitimate the preemptive use of force in customary international law.[7]

EFFECT OF THE UNITED NATIONS CHARTER

However, with the founding of the United Nations, the legitimacy of the use of force by individual states under international law has been substantially narrowed. The Charter of the UN states in its Preamble that the UN is established "to save succeeding generations from the scourge of war";

---

[5] Letter from Secretary of State Daniel Webster to Lord Ashburton of August 6, 1842, set forth in Moore, John Bassett, A Digest of International Law, Vol. II (1906), at 412.

[6] Letter from Mr. Webster to Mr. Fox of April 24, 1841, 29 British and Foreign State Papers 1129, 1138 (1857), quoted in Damrosch, Lori, International Law: Cases and Materials (2001), at 923.

[7] In its advisory opinion on the Legality of the Threat or Use of Nuclear Weapons, the International Court of Justice stated that "[t]he submission of the exercise of the right of self-defence to the conditions of necessity and proportionality is a rule of customary international law." 1996 I.C.J. Reports para. 41.

and its substantive provisions obligate the Member States of the UN to "settle their international disputes by peaceful means" (Article 2(3)) and to "refrain in their international relations from the threat or use of force against the territorial integrity or political independence of any State, or in any manner inconsistent with the Purposes of the United Nations" (Article 2(4)). In place of the traditional right of states to use force, the Charter creates a system of collective security in which the Security Council is authorized to "determine the existence of any threat to the peace, breach of the peace, or act of aggression" and to "decide what measures shall be taken ... to maintain international peace and security" (Article 39).

Although nominally outlawing most uses of force in international relations by individual States, the UN Charter does recognize a right of nations to use force for the purpose of self-defense. Article 51 of the Charter provides:

> Nothing in the present Charter shall impair the inherent right of individual or collective self-defence if an armed attack occurs against a Member of the United Nations, until the Security Council has taken measures necessary to maintain international peace and security.[8]

The exact scope of this right of self-defense, however, has been the subject of ongoing debate. Read literally, Article 51's articulation of the right seems to preclude the preemptive use of force by individual states or groupings of states and to reserve such uses of force exclusively to the Security Council. Measures in self-defense, in this understanding, are legitimate only after an armed attack has already occurred.[9]

Others contend that Article 51 should not be construed so narrowly and that "it would be a travesty of the purposes of the Charter to compel a defending state to allow its assailant to deliver the first, and perhaps fatal,

---

[8] United Nations Charter, Article 51.

[9] This reading of Article 51 finds support in the decision of the International Court of Justice in Military and Paramilitary Activities in and Against Nicaragua (Nicaragua v. United States of America), 1986 I.C.J. Reports p. 14. The Court decided the case on the basis of customary international law rather than Articles 2(4) and 51 of the UN Charter but found the latter to "correspond, in essentials, to those found in customary international law." The gravamen of the Court's ruling was that in customary international law as well as Article 51, the use of force in self-defense is justified only in response to an armed attack: ... [F]or one State to use force against another ... is regarded as lawful, by way of exception, only when the wrongful act provoking the response was an armed attack .... In the view of the Court, under international law in force today – whether customary international law or that of the United Nations system – States do not have a right of "collective" armed response to acts which do not constitute an "armed attack."
Id. para. 211.

blow ...."[10] To read Article 51 literally, it is said, "is to protect the aggressor's right to the first strike."[11] Consequently, to avoid this result, some assert that Article 51 recognizes the "inherent right of individual or collective self-defence" as it developed in customary international law prior to adoption of the Charter and preserves it intact. The reference to that right not being impaired "if an armed attack occurs against a Member of the United Nations," it is said, merely emphasizes one important situation where that right may be exercised but does not exclude or exhaust other possibilities.[12]

In further support of this view, it is argued that the literal construction of Article 51 simply ignores the reality that the Cold War and other political considerations have often paralyzed the Security Council and that, in practice, states have continued to use force preemptively at times in the UN era and the international community has continued to evaluate the legitimacy of those uses by the traditional constraints of necessity and proportionality. Examples used to illustrate these contentions have included the following:

- In 1962 President Kennedy, in response to photographic evidence that the Soviet Union was installing medium range missiles in Cuba capable of hitting the United State, imposed a naval "quarantine" on Cuba in order "to interdict ... the delivery of offensive weapons and associated material."[13] Although President Kennedy said that the purpose of the quarantine was "to defend the security of the United States," the U.S. did not rely on the legal concept of self-defense either as articulated in Article 51 or otherwise as a justification for its actions. Abram Chayes the Legal Adviser to the State Department at that time, later explained the decision not to rely on that justification as follows:

---

[10] Statement by Sir Humphrey Waldock, quoted in Roberts, Guy, "The Counterproliferation Self- Help Paradigm: A Legal Regime for Enforcing the Norm Prohibiting the Proliferation of Weapons of Mass Destruction," 27 Denver Journal of International Law and Policy 483, 513 (1999).

[11] Id.

[12] Simma, Bruno, ed., The Charter of the United Nations: A Commentary (1994), at 51. This contention finds some support in the advisory opinion of the International Court of Justice in Legality of the Threat or Use of Nuclear Weapons, 1996 I.C.J. Reports para. 96-97. In passing on the question of whether it might ever be legal for a nation to use nuclear weapons, the Court refused to construe Article 51 or customary international law to preclude "the use of nuclear weapons by a State in an extreme circumstance of self-defence, in which its very survival would be at stake." The Court's decision did not specifically deal with the question of preemptive attack. But it seems to give support to an expansive understanding of what might be permissible in instances of extreme necessity.

[13] Proclamation 3504, 27 Fed. Reg. 10401 (October 25, 1962).

In retrospect ... I think the central difficulty with the Article 51 argument was that it seemed to trivialize the whole effort at legal justification. No doubt the phrase "armed attack" must be construed broadly enough to permit some anticipatory response. But it is a very different matter to expand it to include threatening deployments or demonstrations that do not have imminent attack as their purpose or probable outcome. To accept that reading is to make the occasion for forceful response essentially a question for unilateral national decision that would not only be formally unreviewable, but not subject to intelligent criticism, either .... Whenever a nation believed that interests, which in the heat and pressure of a crisis it is prepared to characterize as vital, were threatened, its use of force in response would become permissible .... In this sense, I believe that an Article 51 defence would have signalled that the United States did not take the legal issues involved very seriously, that in its view the situation was to be governed by national discretion, not international law.[14]

- In 1967 Israel launched a preemptive attack on Egypt and other Arab states after President Nasser had moved his army across the Sinai toward Israel, forced the UN to withdraw its peacekeeping force from the Sinai border, and closed the port of Aqaba to Israeli shipping, and after Syria, Iraq, Jordan, and Saudi Arabia all began moving troops to the Israeli borders. In six days it routed Egypt and its Arab allies and had occupied the Sinai Peninsula, the West Bank, and the Gaza Strip. Israel claimed its attack was defensive in nature and necessary to forestall an Arab invasion. Both the Security Council and the General Assembly rejected proposals to condemn Israel for its "aggressive" actions.[15]

- On June 7, 1981, Israel bombed and destroyed a nuclear reactor under construction in Iraq. Asserting that Iraq considered itself to be in a state of war with Israel, that it had participated in the three wars with Israel in 1948, 1967, and 1973, that it continued to deny that Israel has a right to exist, and that its nuclear program was for the purpose of developing weapons capable of destroying Israel, Israel claimed that "in removing this terrible nuclear threat to its

---

[14] See Chayes, A., The Cuban Missile Crisis (1974), at 63-64, quoted in Carter, Barry, and Trimble, Phillip, International Law (1999), at 1241-42.

[15] The Security Council, instead, adopted Resolution 242 calling on Israel to withdraw from the territories and for the termination of all claims or states of belligerency and the acknowledgment of the territorial integrity and the right of every State in the region to live in peace.

existence, Israel was only exercising its legitimate right of self-defense within the meaning of this term in international law and as preserved also under the United Nations Charter."[16] Nonetheless, the Security Council unanimously "condemn[ed] the military attack by Israel in clear violation of the Charter of the United Nations and the norms of international conduct" and urged the payment of "appropriate redress."[17]

CURRENT SITUATION

Thus, in both theory and practice the preemptive use of force appears to have a home in current international law; but its boundaries are not wholly determinate. Its clearest legal foundation is in Chapter VII of the UN Charter. Under Article 39 the Security Council has the authority to determine the existence not only of breaches of the peace or acts of aggression that have already occurred but also of threats to the peace; and under Article 42 it has the authority to "take such action by air, sea, or land forces as may be necessary to maintain or restore international peace and security." These authorities clearly seem to encompass the possibility of the preemptive use of force. As a consequence, the preemptive use of force by the United States against Iraq or any other sovereign nation pursuant to an appropriate authorization by the Security Council would seem to be consonant with international law. Less clear is whether international law currently allows the preemptive use of force by a nation or group of nations without Security Council authorization. That would seem to be permissible only if Article 51 is not read literally but expansively to preserve as lawful the use of force in self-defense as traditionally allowed in customary international law. As noted, the construction of Article 51 remains a matter of debate. But so construed, Article 51 would not preclude the preemptive use of force by the U.S. against Iraq or other sovereign nations. To be lawful, however, such uses of force would need to meet the traditional requirements of necessity and proportionality.

If customary international law governing the preemptive use of force does remain valid, a primary difficulty still remains of determining what situations meet the test of necessity. As illustrated in the examples listed above, that requirement is most easily met when an armed attack is clearly imminent, as in the case of the Arab-Israeli War of 1967. But beyond such obvious situations, as Abram Chayes argued, the judgment of necessity

---

[16] 20 ILM 996 (July, 1981) (excerpts from Security Council debate).
[17] Id. at 993 (S/RES/487 adopted on June 19, 1981).

becomes increasingly subjective; and there is at present no consensus either in theory or practice about whether the possession or development of weapons of mass destruction by a rogue state justifies the preemptive use of force. Most analysts recognize that if overwhelmingly lethal weaponry is possessed by a nation willing to use that weaponry directly or through surrogates, some kind of anticipatory self-defense may be a matter of national survival; and many contend that international law ought, if it does not already do so, to allow for the preemptive use of force in that situation. But many states and analysts are decidedly reluctant to legitimate the preemptive use of force even in that situation on the grounds the justification can easily be abused. Moreover, it remains a fact that the international community judged Israel's destruction of Iraq's nuclear reactor site in 1981 to be an aggressive act rather than an act of self-defense; and there has not been any further refinement of the characteristics that might make analogous situations meet the test of necessity. Given this fluidity, the legality under international law of a preemptive attack on Iraq or another sovereign nation by the U.S. in the current situation, if done apart from authorization by the Security Council, may not be able to be judged with any certainty at the outset. Moreover, it may ultimately have the effect of shaping what is deemed to be a lawful preemptive use of force.

INDEX

A

Afghanistan, 5, 12, 14, 39, 42
Africa Growth and Opportunity Act, 28
Africa, 10, 12, 17, 18, 27-29, 34
African Development Fund, 32
African Growth and Opportunity Act, 27
African Union, 18
agriculture, 27, 29
alliance partners, 37
allies, 4, 7, 8, 12-14, 17-23, 26, 29, 35-38, 40-43, 45, 63, 70
al-Qaida, 12
American forces overseas, 42
American internationalism, 8
Annan, Kofi, 34
ANZUS Treaty, 37
armed hostility, 55
arms control, 21
Army, 56
ASEAN, 37
Asia, 12, 16, 29, 37, 39, 40, 42
Asia-Pacific Economic Cooperation, 37
Australia, 28, 37
authoritarian systems, 10

B

Battle of the Coral Sea, 37
Belgrade, 10
bilateral relations, 10, 16, 38, 44
bilateral trade, 38
biotechnology, 34
bioterror, 14
border controls, 14
Brazil, 17
Bush, President George W., 6, 7, 9, 11, 15, 19, 25, 31, 35, 41, 47, 59, 60, 65

C

Canada, 17, 28, 35, 67
Carter, 70
Central America, 28, 61-63
chemical weapons, 20
children, 3, 9, 33, 34
Chile, 17, 28
China, 27, 30, 37, 39, 40
CIA, 49, 50
civil wars, 18, 44
coalitions, 17, 18, 21, 35, 36
Cold War, 19, 22, 36, 38, 42, 69
Colombia, 17
commerce, 33, 38, 40
Communist Party, 39

competition, 28, 29, 37, 41
Congress, 28, 41, 49, 56, 57, 60
Constitution, 56
corruption, 5, 16, 25, 26, 32
counterproliferation, 21
counterterrorism, 20, 37, 39, 47-50, 52
covert action, 63
Cuba, 60, 63, 64, 69
Cuban Missile Crisis, 22, 64, 70
Cubans, 64

D

Declaration of Independence, 10
Defense Intelligence Agency, 52
Defense Ministerial of the Americas, 17
democracy, 3-5, 8, 10, 16-18, 34, 38
Department of Defense, 13, 42, 48, 51
Department of Homeland Security, 13, 48-51
Department of State, 44
deterrence, 19, 22, 41, 42
developing countries, 26, 28, 30, 33, 34
development aid, 25, 31
development assistance, 5, 31-33
development projects, 33
Diaz, President Adolfo, 62
diplomacy, 13, 21, 43
Director of Central Intelligence, 43, 47, 48, 50
Dominican Republic, 62, 63
drug cartels, 5, 17
drug trafficking, 17
dumping, 29

E

economic development, 16, 33
economic freedom, 3-5, 8, 18, 25, 32, 38

economic growth, 8, 25-27, 29, 31, 33
education, 25, 26, 32-34, 44
emergency management systems, 13
emerging markets, 26, 27
energy security, 29
espionage, 29
Ethiopia, 18
ethnic minorities, 17
Europe, 10, 12, 26, 35, 40, 42
European allies, 17, 18, 36, 38
European Union (EU), 28, 35, 36

F

fair trading practices, 29
Federal Bureau of Investigation (FBI), 13, 47, 48-51
financing of terrorism, 12
foreign assistance, 10
foreign policy, 36, 59-61
free markets, 5, 8, 25
free trade agreements, 28
Free Trade Area of the Americas, 27
free trade, 5, 8, 25-29, 34
freedom, 3-5, 7-10, 13, 16, 18, 19, 25, 27, 32, 35, 38, 39, 42, 45

G

genocide, 13
Germany, 15
global economy, 26, 29
global fund, 34
global security, 4, 26, 44
global terrorism, 8, 12-14
global war, 38, 51
grants, 33
greenhouse gas(es), 29, 30
Group of Seven, 26
Guatemala, 63
Gulf War, 20, 61

Index

H

Haiti, 62
health care, 32, 33
health, 17, 25, 26, 28, 32-34, 39, 44
HIV/AIDS, 5, 28, 33, 34, 39
homeland security, 13, 21, 43
human dignity, 5, 8-10, 15, 17
human rights, 3, 10, 32, 39
human suffering, 15, 16
humanitarian assistance, 16, 32
hunger, 34
Hussein, Saddam, 65

I

imminent threat, 22
India, 16, 30, 37-40
Indonesia, 17
intelligence community, 43
intelligence infrastructure, 17
international aid, 5
international community, 4, 12, 13, 29, 69, 72
international cooperation, 10, 30, 44
International Criminal Court (ICC), 44
International Development Association (IDA), 32, 33
international financial system, 12
international institutions, 10, 18, 35, 44
International Labor Organization, 29
international law, 20, 22, 55, 60, 65-71
International Monetary Fund (IMF), 27
international organizations, 14
international relationships, 14, 15
international terrorism, 13
international trade, 28
international treaties, 20
Iran, 20, 63
Iraq, 20, 56, 59-61, 65, 70-72

Israel, 16, 70, 72
Israeli-Palestinian conflict, 16

J

Japan, 26, 37, 56
Jordan, 28, 70

K

Kennedy, President John F., 64, 69
Kenya, 18
Korean War, 61
Kosovo, 61

L

Latin America, 10, 17, 63
law enforcement, 4, 12, 17, 43, 44, 50, 51

M

market access, 28
Mexico, 17, 25, 28
Middle East, 12
military air strikes, 64
military forces, 21, 23, 36, 59, 60, 62, 63
military/paramilitary forces, 63
Millennium Challenge Account, 5, 32
missile programs, 39
Mitchell Committee, 16
Morocco, 28
Moscow Treaty on Strategic Reductions, 38
multilateral development banks, 32, 33

N

narcotics trafficking, 17
narcotics, 17
National Security Agency, 51

National Security Council, 13
NATO-Russia Council, 38
New Millennium Challenge, 5
New Zealand, 37
Nicaragua, 62, 68
Nigeria, 18
Nixon, President, 57
non-governmental organizations, 14, 44
nonproliferation, 21, 40
North America, 12
North Atlantic Treaty Organization (NATO), 5, 35, 36, 38, 61
North Korea, 20
nuclear weapons, 19, 20, 69

O

open markets, 17, 25, 29
Operation Enduring Freedom, 37
Organization of American States (OAS), 5, 17

P

Pakistan, 16
Palestine, 16
Palestinian state, 16
Panama Canal, 62
Panama, 62
Philippines, 37
piracy, 13
poverty, 5, 6, 9, 17, 25-28, 31, 32
preemptive actions, 23
preemptive options, 23
private sector, 13, 27, 32, 33
productivity growth, 32
property rights, 28
public record, 63

Q

quarantine, 64, 69

R

race, 7, 31
reform agenda, 32
Republic of Korea, 10, 37
rogue states, 20, 21, 22
Roosevelt, President Franklin D., 62
rule of law, 9, 16, 17, 26, 28, 32, 40
Russia, 4, 19, 27, 37, 38, 40, 61

S

Saudi Arabia, 70
Secretary of State, 60, 66, 67
September 11, 5, 23, 35, 37, 40, 45, 47, 49, 50, 55
Singapore, 28, 37
slavery, 13
South America, 12
South Korea, 37
Soviet Union, 19, 20, 38, 64, 69
Soviets, 64
State Department, 44, 69
Summit of the Americas, 17

T

Taiwan Relations Act, 40
Taiwan, 10, 27, 40
Taliban, 12
tax policies, 26
terrorism, 8, 11-14, 20, 37-39, 42, 44, 45, 47, 48, 50, 51
terrorist financing, 4
terrorist networks, 5
terrorist organizations, 12, 17, 50
terrorists, 3, 4, 5, 7, 11-14, 17, 20-23, 43, 48, 65
Thailand, 37
totalitarianism, 3
trade negotiations, 27, 29
Trade Promotion Authority, 28
trade, 5, 8, 20, 25-29, 33, 35, 38, 39
Truman Administration, 13

Index

U

U.N. Conference on Financing for Development in Monterrey, 31
U.N. Framework Convention for international cooperation, 30
U.S. assistance, 17
U.S. infrastructure, 42
U.S. military force, 59, 60, 63
U.S.-Australian alliance, 37
United Nations Charter, 57, 65, 67, 68, 71
United Nations, 5, 14, 57, 61, 65, 67-69, 71
use of force, 19, 55-57, 59-61, 65-68, 70, 71

V

violence, 4, 9, 11, 15-17

W

War Powers Resolution (WPR), 57
war, 4, 6, 11-14, 16-18, 31, 35, 37-39, 42, 44, 51, 55-57, 60, 61, 66, 67, 70
weapons of mass destruction (WMD), 4, 5, 8, 12, 20-23, 38, 65, 72
World Bank, 16, 32-34
World Trade Organization (WTO), 5, 27-29, 38-40
World War I, 31, 56
World War II, 31, 56
WTO intellectual property rules, 28